Praise for *Same Life, New Story*

"With her customary skill, wisdom, humor, and practical way of dealing with life, Jan Silvious has given us *Same Life, New Story*. If you've ever thought, *I'm sick o' me . . . I don't like who I am or what I've become*, this is the book for you. Jan uses her own story to help *you* with yours, and she weaves ten women from the Bible into our stories, showing us how God changed their struggles and fears into blessings. I love Jan Silvious and have found everything she says helps me in some area of my journey. This book is a winner, Jan. Congratulations!"

—LUCI SWINDOLL
AUTHOR AND WOF® SPEAKER

"Jan Silvious is one of the wisest women I know—I think the only *book* I've underlined more than *Same Life, New Story* is my Bible!"

—LISA HARPER
AUTHOR AND WOF® SPEAKER

"One of the things I love most about Jan is her ability to help me understand my own life. With charming wit and insightful wisdom, she shines the light of God's Word on what is true, good or bad, and shows us how to grow. In this study of the lives of ten women whose stories we may feel we know, Jan gives us a fresh look at their lives and helps us see our own."

—SHEILA WALSH
WOF® SPEAKER AND AUTHOR,
THE SHELTER OF GOD'S PROMISES

"When Jan Silvious speaks, I lean in and listen! With the voice of wisdom, common sense, and experience, Jan's practical approach to applying God's Word to life helps put the modern-day woman on the road toward maturity. In *Same Life, New Story* Jan reveals that our setbacks are really setups that launch us into becoming what God desires us to be."

—BABBIE MASON
AWARD-WINNING SINGER, SONGWRITER,
AUTHOR, AND CONFERENCE SPEAKER

"There are only a couple of books that make my *must* list in any year. Jan's books are *always* on that very short list because she combines ancient truths in relatable, honest-to-goodness girl-friend language that allows us all to access life-changing concepts. Complex truth in simple wrapping. If you've been wondering why your life isn't as fulfilling as you had hoped or why it just isn't working, I highly commend *Same Life, New Story* to you. Once you understand the power of your internal dialog, not only to frame your circumstance but to impact your choices and literally narrow or widen your options, you will see why this book is a soul necessity. Give yourself the gift of perspective. Jan Silvious's writing can change yours."

—ANITA RENFROE
COMEDIAN AND AUTHOR

SAME LIFE, NEW STORY

CHANGE YOUR PERSPECTIVE to CHANGE YOUR LIFE

JAN SILVIOUS

THOMAS NELSON
Since 1798

NASHVILLE   DALLAS   MEXICO CITY   RIO DE JANEIRO

Published in Nashville, Tennessee, by Thomas Nelson. Thomas Nelson is a registered trademark of Thomas Nelson, Inc.

Thomas Nelson, Inc. titles may be purchased in bulk for educational, business, fund-raising, or sales promotional use. For information, please e-mail SpecialMarkets@ThomasNelson.com.

Unless otherwise noted, Scripture quotations are taken from the New Century Version®. © 2005 by Thomas Nelson, Inc. Used by permission. All rights reserved.

Scripture quotations marked AMP are from the Amplified Bible, © 1962, 1964, 1965, 1987 by The Lockman Foundation. Used by permission.

Scripture quotations marked NASB are from the New American Standard Bible®, © The Lockman Foundation 1960, 1962, 1963, 1968, 1971, 1972, 1973, 1975, 1977, 1995. Used by permission.

Scripture quotations marked NIV are from the Holy Bible, New International Version®. © 1973, 1978, 1984 by Biblica, Inc.™ Used by permission of Zondervan. All rights reserved worldwide. www.zondervan.com.

Scripture quotations marked NKJV are from the New King James Version®. © 1982 by Thomas Nelson, Inc. Used by permission. All rights reserved.

Scripture quotations marked MSG are from *The Message* by Eugene H. Peterson. © 1993, 1994, 1995, 1996, 2000, 2001, 2002. Used by permission of NavPress Publishing Group. All rights reserved.

Scripture quotations marked NLT are from the Holy Bible, New Living Translation. © 1996. Used by permission of Tyndale House Publishers, Inc., Wheaton, Illinois 60189. All rights reserved.

Stories from individuals in this book have been used with their permission.

Library of Congress Cataloging-in-Publication Data

Silvious, Jan, 1944–
  Same life, new story : change your perspective to change your life / Jan Silvious.
     p. cm.
  Includes bibliographical references.
  ISBN 978-0-7852-2819-6 (pbk.)
  1. Christian women—Religious life. 2. Women in the Bible. I. Title.
  BS575.S445 2010
  248.8'43—dc22

                                                                    2010039567

Printed in the United States of America

11 12 13 14 15 16 RRD 6 5 4 3 2 1

To Lynda Elliott and Pam Gillaspie

You have been my Aaron and Hur.
I'm deeply grateful.

Contents

Naomi found a life worth living after sowing years
of bitterness.

Leah changed her theme in the midst of a
humiliating situation.

Rahab saved her family and her own neck as a result of
acting on the truth.

Deborah answered "I can" when God called her to lead in a
culture not affirming to women.

Hannah faced infertility and depression but resisted the
role of Drama Queen.

Acknowledgments

Susie, Karen, Jean, Laura, Judy, Pam, Pat, Brenda, and Cindy—we birthed this concept together. Our bond is great.

Susan, Cecile, Margaret, Wanda, Karen, and Debbie—I've seen each of you write new stories. Your new lives make me smile.

Charlie, David, Sandi, Lauren, Luke, Jon, Aaron, Heather, Rachel, Ben, and Bekah—you are the lead characters in my personal play. I love you.

Sandy Smith—you always pray me across the finish line.

And Debbie Wickwire, Mary Hollingsworth, Rebecca Price—what a team! I'm grateful.

Introduction

IF YOU CHANGE YOUR STORY, YOU CAN CHANGE YOUR LIFE

I had always felt life first as a story. And if there is a story, there is a storyteller.

—G. K. Chesterton

I wish there were some wonderful place
Called the Land of Beginning Again,
Where all our mistakes and
All our heartaches
And all our selfish grief
Could be dropped like a shabby old coat at the door,
And never be put on again.[1]

—Louisa Fletcher

Do you like the life you're living? As Dr. Phil says, "How's it working for you?" Do you wish you could somehow stay the same and yet be different? When you look at the big picture of your life, does it appear good and hopeful and exciting? Or do you need a different perspective? Do you wish you could wipe the slate clean and get a fresh start on an old story that somehow has not turned out as you had planned or hoped?

If you have ever said, "I wish I could just begin again," then sweet friend, I have good news for you. There is a place of beginning again. This place may not look exactly as you *want* it to look or think it *should* look, but it is a place to start over. It most often comes with a new perspective and a new way of thinking that use your past experiences as a springboard to a different way of living. Sounds too simple, doesn't it? It is simple in many ways, and yet the effects of changed thinking are profound.

Think of your life as a story—one you have been writing since birth. And depending on your age, you have filled up a number of pages, some fuller than others, of course. Some pages are good, others are not so good, but it's important to remember that the story is not finished. If you are breathing and alive, there are always new blank pages on which to write. You *can* find a new way of thinking and a new way of speaking to yourself and others that will change the course of your life.

Maybe you are thinking, *But I am just who I am. Do you really think I can write a new story?*

Yes, I know you can, and I know it will alter your life and the lives of those around you for the good.

Or you may be one of the life-is-good girls. Things are going along just as you like them right now, and you do not want to think about writing anything new or different into your life book. I understand. There is a time and a place for new things to begin, and perhaps that time is not right now, but I would encourage you to keep the idea close by because paragraphs and chapters in our lives will often need editing or revising. Even when you are living the "good life," there are people, places, and things that might need to be seen in a different light.

There are many more adventures to be had, tales to be told, and stories to record in your life, no matter where you are on the age spectrum. If you have just hit adulthood, welcome to reality. If you are just starting into your middle years, it could be time to take a second look and alter some of your thinking. If you are living in "the rest of your years," you may have been telling the same old story much too long. As a result, the eyes of the people around you may be glazing over instead of locking into what you have to say.

> *There is no greater agony than bearing an untold story inside of you.*
> —Maya Angelou

Wherever you are, a new story is just waiting to be written, and you are the only one who can write it. Do not look to the people in your life—beloved or estranged. *They* are not required to be different so *you* can be different. It is all about *you*. It is all about what you think about them, not what they think about you. It is all about what you say to yourself about them, not what they say to you about themselves. It is all up to you! The story is yours to create, and it is yours to tell.

Some of us have stories we love, some have stories we hate, and some have stories that seem so unremarkable they have no emotion about them at all. No matter where you find yourself on that continuum, stop and think for a moment: today you lived a page in your story. Was it a good day, a bad day, or a ho-hum day? Whatever your answer, it is amazing to realize that this day has been part of the story you are writing. It is a day when God was present and involved, whether you recognized it or not. It may have been a day when your *backstory* (the circumstances of your life up to this day) was influencing how you thought and what you did. Or it may be a day that the *sidestory* (the diversions and dramas that keep us from seeing the big picture) held your attention captive.

Maybe you did not realize it, but good day or bad day, boring day or exciting day, there is far more going on in your story than you can imagine, and God has much more to do with it than you might dream.

This is a book about a story—your story. This is a book about writing a new story and discovering that the authentic principal character—the hero—is you.

This is also a story about God, the God who was "in the beginning" (Gen. 1:1), and yet is very present in every moment of today and in all the days to come. This is a book about how we see God's pen strokes in the chapters of our lives. They can be easy to miss but, hopefully, as you learn to tell a new story, His part will become clearer. He may act as your Herald, who calls you to a new adventure. He may be your Mentor, who guides you and teaches you. Or He may be a Threshold Guardian, who prevents you from going in a certain direction. But you can be sure He is always in the story in one important role or another.

It is a story, too, about ancient people in Scripture who lived lives that parallel ours in many uncanny ways. Some of them had great stories, and some . . . well, some of them lived stories that were not so great. But after all was said and done, their stories live on, and so will ours. Oh, we will never make it into the Scriptures as Sarah, Martha, Jezebel, and Delilah did, but people somewhere are reading our stories right now. And even when we are gone, those people will remember things about us and the stories we have told with our lives.

When you begin writing your new story, you won't be facing a blank sheet of paper and wondering what and how you are going to do this. I'm going to walk with you all the way. We are women, living life and wanting to tell the very best stories we can. Our stories will be about *truth, vulnerability*, and *transparency*—all words that can give even the bravest wordsmiths writer's cramp. Still, it will be a journey you will love once you take the first step. Just as writers who are starting new books, we will begin by putting the first word on the page, then the first sentence, and the first paragraph. And we are not going to panic if at first it does not read exactly the way we want it to. Just hang in there and know there is always more to tell, and you will always have editing privileges.

—Jan Silvious

P. S. In order to make this book as self-contained and user-friendly as possible, I included many of the actual scriptures that tell these biblical tales. You may still want to use your own Bible. I would recommend you choose a personal journal in which to begin writing your new story—it could change your life!

Chapter 1

REALIZE IT'S TIME
TO GET A LIFE AND TELL
A NEW STORY

*We must be willing to let go of the life we have planned,
so as to have the life that is waiting for us.*

—E. M. Forster

Naomi

Naomi found a life worth living after
sowing years of bitterness.

THE BOOK OF RUTH

It's true: Naomi's story was a tragedy. Due to famine in her home-land of Judah, she and her husband, Elimelech, and their two sons, Mahlon and Kilion, had to move to Moab, a foreign country with false gods, and set up housekeeping among strangers.

Then Elimelech suddenly died, leaving Naomi with her two sons. Mahlon and Kilion married two women from Moab named Ruth and Orpah, and things seemed to be getting better as Naomi looked forward to being a grandmother and living out her life in peace with her family.

After they had been in Moab about ten years, Mahlon and Kilion both died too. Then Naomi, distraught from her devastating losses, was alone in a foreign land with just her daughters-in-law. Now what? How could an older woman survive in Moab with no husband and no sons to care for her? It was not Ruth and Orpah's responsibility to take care of her—they needed to return to their own families for help. What could she do?

Naomi's story had changed drastically, and she had no idea how to write the next part. Can you relate? Have you ever been there?

My grandmother lived thirty-six years. Her story was short compared to most. She married as a girl of seventeen and gave birth to ten children over the next eighteen years. After her last baby was born, she died of childbirth fever, a common affliction of her day. Her story probably would not have ended that way had she been living now, but during her time on earth, giving birth, which has always been hazardous, was often deadly. Her life ended abruptly with no time to say good-bye.

Her children were bewildered. Her husband was broken, faced with a brood of motherless children, and the love of his life—his North Star—was gone. The plot of their family's story had taken a nasty twist they had not anticipated, but life for the rest of them had to go on.

The day he buried his wife, my grandfather drew his children into a circle and told them they were all going to face changes. They would have to pull together and help each other as never before. Some of them were too young to understand what he was saying, but the older ones knew what he meant. Life as they had known it was over.

While I can only imagine how bleak their whole existence must have looked at that pivotal moment, the truth was, my grandmother's strong influence remained with them all from that tragic day forward.

I was born into this hardy family but did not know the struggles they had faced until I was an adult. As a child I knew that my mother had an incredible bond with her sisters and brothers. I never knew them to be divided by arguments or petty jealousies. Through thick and thin, sickness and accidents, foreign wars and family reunions, births and deaths, they lived together with kindness, caring, and mutual support. Their mother had written her story while she could. Through her sacrificial life, her children learned what she wanted them to know. If she had lived another thirty-six years, I cannot imagine they would have turned out any better.

I often think of my grandmother and wonder if I have lived as well as she did in her brief stay here. The fact that I am alive and have breath gives me options, though, that she did not have. Although it will be up to those who come behind us to interpret what we have written and to make judgments about the legacies we leave, the *writing of it* is in our hands. It is up to us to write stories worth reading and remembering.

The part that is up to us is how well we respond to the events and circumstances that happen in our lives. Some of my grandmother's children had to live in different homes for a few years. It was hard for them, but they managed to see it in a way that propelled them forward. They did not allow it to stop them or make them into victims. No matter what they went through, they lived with optimism and strength.

Writing our life stories well is huge. Choosing not to linger in a bad scenario, but choosing to move on to new pages and chapters or maybe even a whole new book, is what marks a good life—a life with a meaning and influence.

If we live with an eye on the fact that God knows when and where we live in the grand scheme of things—in fact, He placed us precisely here—it is easier to relax into our futures, the unwritten parts of our stories. We will always live the same life, but as long as we have breath, we can write a new story. As long as there is life, God's imprint is on the pages. We can know there is a bigger story going on around us, and we can reach beyond this moment to see the more. Even if, for now, things seem bleak, unfair, and ungracious, there is hope because there is always more to your story.

From Pleasantness to Bitterness

Naomi, a prominent woman in Scripture whose name means "pleasantness," is a significant character in a drama that seemed to go so very wrong. In fact, because of her sad life she eventually declared she had changed her name to Mara, which means "bitterness."

It is hard to believe she ever imagined there could be more to her life. She lived during a barren time in the history of Israel—the time of the judges, which is described as a time when "everyone was doing what was right in his own eyes" (Judg. 17:6 NKJV), and living was hard. There was a famine in the land, which caused Naomi, her husband, Elimelech, and their two sons, Kilion and Mahlon, to pack their belongings and leave their home in Bethlehem. They went to Moab, a land where the people worshipped many false gods, but at least there was food in Moab.

We do not know if things got much better for them there, but what we do know is that, before long, Elimelech died. And while that was certainly tragic, Naomi still had her boys. The sons married Moabite women, and they all lived together in Moab for ten years. Sadly, though, both of her sons then died. Naomi was bereft. Distraught. Depressed. Her life was turned upside down, and her story took a disastrous turn. She had no husband, no sons, and only daughters-in-law in a strange land. It could not have looked much worse for an Israelite woman of Naomi's age. I can only imagine the sorrow and despair that surrounded her. What would she do? Her daughters-in-law had their own families and surely were not obligated to take care of her. They were still young enough to remarry and have children. But not Naomi.

One day, in the midst of her despair, a message came that gave Naomi a little glimmer of hope. She heard that the famine had been broken in Israel, and the Lord had at last given His people food. So the tired, grieving Israelite woman packed her meager belongings to leave Moab and return home to Bethlehem in Judah:

> Naomi and her daughters-in-law left the place where they had lived and started back to the land of Judah. But Naomi said to her two daughters-in-law, "Go back home, each of you to your own mother's house. May the LORD be as kind to you as you have been to me and my sons who are now dead. May the LORD give you another happy home and a new husband." (Ruth 1:7–9)

Naomi knew her daughters-in-law could start over again. A new beginning was possible for them, but I wonder if it ever occurred to her that she could begin again too? She probably thought she had lived her life. The family she expected to grow old with was gone. The future held no happy expectation of grandchildren or even the comfort of living among old friends. She had nothing in Moab. So she was going to do the only thing she knew to do—return home to her own people and relatives. She said farewell to the only connections she had in Moab.

"When Naomi kissed the women good-bye, they began to cry out loud. They said to her, 'No, we want to go with you to your people'" (vv. 9–10). But Naomi tried to send the girls home to their own families. She even played on their emotions by saying, "I cannot give birth to more sons to give you new husbands" (v. 11). Then she went to an extreme thought. Even if she conceived children that very night, she could not ask the girls to wait for them to grow up. She did not want them to live without husbands, so she said, "Don't do that, my daughters. My life is much too sad for you to share, because the LORD has been against me!" (v. 13).

Naomi had titled her old story "Too Sad." She had even come up with that outlandish scenario—a new husband, new children, and daughters-in-law frozen in time to wait for Naomi's future sons to grow up! She had concocted an impossible plot so she could go back to Bethlehem and give her daughters-in-law an "out." She only saw the future one possible way, and the girls were not part of it. She had one plan in mind, and they were not included. As so often happens, however, life threw her a curve. Just when she thought she had her sad existence all figured out, one of those girls did not do what Naomi expected. Ruth did not take her "out." And the plot took a left turn.

> The women cried together out loud again. Then Orpah kissed
> her mother-in-law Naomi good-bye, but Ruth held on to her
> tightly.
>
> Naomi said to Ruth, "Look, your sister-in-law is going
> back to her own people and her own gods. Go back with her."
>
> But Ruth said, "Don't beg me to leave you or to stop

following you. Where you go, I will go. Where you live, I will live. Your people will be my people, and your God will be my God. And where you die, I will die, and there I will be buried. I ask the LORD to punish me terribly if I do not keep this promise: Not even death will separate us." (vv. 14–17)

Naomi was given a daughter—a daughter who vowed to stay with her until death. She had no idea about this new story line. Life had been hard, but now something wonderful had happened. What would her story be now? How would this new chapter develop?

We All Live Many Stories

Most of us live several stories in a lifetime. That is the way God works so often. What starts out looking like a scenario with limited possibilities and little future can be just *one* of the chapters we live. That is the beauty of knowing that God is writing the main plot of your life story even while you meander aimlessly through side dramas and subplots. He is there all the time, patiently nudging you back toward His ultimate plan for you.

For years I lived in the backstory of my early marriage. I met my husband on a blind date in college. We fell in love, married, and had a baby boy. I liked that part of the story and loved living it, but within six months of our baby's birth, my husband was taken away to fly a helicopter in the jungles of Vietnam. I hated that chapter. It was not what I wanted. We tried to make the most of it. We wrote letters to one another every day (we had no Internet then). We endured all the things every other military couple was enduring at that critical moment in history. We were making the most of a tough situation, but I was depressed and became even more so when he came home. We had missed the entire third year of our marriage, he had lost a most important year in our growing son's life, and both of us had changed significantly. Where was the rightness in all of that?

I felt as if I had awakened angry one day and could not get over it. I had many strings of conversations with myself that seemed to be circular threads that never went anywhere. I was stuck in my mind and could not see a way out of the injustice and loss. You can see I made it a far larger circumstance than it really was by using those big words—*injustice* and *loss*. Although my husband had come home, and ten months later we had another beautiful son, it made no difference to me. I thought I had my story, and I had no idea there was *more*. I just felt trapped in a chapter I did not love, yet I think I *wanted* to love it. I wanted to live it well, but I just did not know how.

I can look back now and recognize when it began to dawn on me that I was stuck. I was twenty-six years old and angry. I knew my life was not working the way I wanted. The dreams were small. We were right in the middle of life, and I was living a fearful existence. My husband had come home from the war alive, and instead of being thrilled and grateful that he had dodged the deadly bullets, I had succumbed to one big *imaginary* bullet that had gone right through my soul. I had become desperately afraid that now *I* would die.

We had two children at that time, and I was scared to death I would pass away from something dreadful and someone else would raise my boys. I saw no greater tragedy than a motherless child and daily struggled with the expectation of death. (For those of you who like to look for the backstory, maybe you can see a clue here, as I did while writing this chapter.) This fear had first surfaced when I was afraid my husband would be killed, and probably even earlier when, as an only child, I lived on hyper-alert, always concerned that something awful would happen to my mother. I always worried that, if something happened to her, I had no one to care for *me*. I had my dad, who was loving and kind, but the idea of being without my mother terrified me. What would happen to me? How would I survive as a motherless child?

Now I had become a mother myself, and I struggled with every perceived danger. Magazine articles on illness and television programs on poor health all held me hostage. I just knew the next paragraph or news flash would identify my cough or small skin lesion as deadly. It was clear I needed to be saved from myself and from my thinking that tended toward the tragic, the sad, and the terminal. My life was one big what-if. My story was stuck on one theme, like the needle on an old, scratched 45 rpm record, and I did not know how to get back on track. I told myself an ongoing narrative of disappointment and depression. Now, years later, I know the root of it was my fear. Despite the gift of wonderful sons, a cute little house, and devoted friends, fear of death haunted me with frightening, tragic scenes, and I believed every word of it. I can only imagine how bored my friends were with my obsession!

My thinking had become a garden full of weeds. I allowed negative thoughts to take root, grow, and multiply. I had no idea I had any responsibility for what was growing or for the misery I felt. I did not have a tragic life; I just had some years I did not like—my young Cinderella dream had been interrupted—while other people's lives had been untouched by the inconvenience of war. That was a disappointment, born of self-pity, that took root in my mind and allowed all sorts of depressing weeds to shoot up. It was not what I had planned, so I did not have a place to file my feelings about the way things had turned out.

Playing Games with God

The answer came to me one night in an encounter with God. (Remember, He also has a story, and it is entwined with ours.) Up to that point I really had not thought much about Him, but this particular night I went to a concert where singer JoAnn Shelton made a statement that changed my life. She was just making the small talk singers sometimes do between songs in a concert. She simply said, "All my life I played games with God, but then I had to get serious." Believe it or not, that was the beginning of the *more* to my story.

I had gone to church all my life, but it seemed to make no difference to me. In fact, I was pretty bored with the things I heard. They seemed so irrelevant. Consequently I played games with God and with myself. I guess that was why I was stunned when the singer spoke the words *played games*. I knew at that exact moment those words were for me. There was a God, and He knew where I was. That was the first glimmer of light in the darkness of my mind, which had been draped in fear for so long. I did not immediately do an about-face, but little by little I began to see that I was not alone, and my life was not without purpose.

"All my life I played games with God, but then I had to get serious."

Later I came to understand there is a God who is bigger

than I am. I came to know Him truly as the Almighty. I learned He has plans for me, and I began to believe nothing comes into my life that is not first "filtered through His sovereign fingers of love."[1] The sky grew brighter. I was being awakened to write a new story. I began to think, *Maybe I can live a different life.*

It was not long after that I read two verses in the Bible that changed my whole perspective: "God has not given us a spirit of fear, but of power and of love and of a sound mind" (2 Tim. 1:7 NKJV). And Jesus said, "I will never leave you nor forsake you" (Heb. 13:5 NKJV). These words lodged in my brain, and I began to see that maybe I no longer had to live as a prisoner of my fears.

Instead I began to think that maybe I did not have to be angry about the loss of time in my marriage. Maybe I did not have to figure out what my life was going to be in the days ahead. Maybe my children would be cared for even if I were not there to mother them. Maybe there was a bigger, more powerful person—a God who had this all under His control—and I could relax a little. Maybe my hyper-vigilance was not valuable anyway. That was the first loosening of the death grip I had on my old way of thinking. It was not totally relinquished, but at that point I began to have a new perspective. It was not about what I could prevent or make happen. It was really about what I *thought* about the events of my life. I was twenty-six years old and *thought* I knew how life was supposed to evolve, but it was not the way I was living.

I needed someone to tell me in the kindest way possible, "Get a life!" It was there for the living, the days were moving on, the clock was ticking, and I was displeased. My children were growing up around me, and I was looking here, there, and yon for ways to get the life I *wanted*. All along, the answer was right there in front of me. I just did not have the wisdom to look.

Writing a New Story Is Up to You

We all have reasons for the stories we write, but sometimes we make our reasons bigger than our own good. Jane was such a woman. She had opportunities to move forward, but she liked her reasons for staying stuck in her backstory. She thought there was purpose in them. She believed she had method to her madness. Do you recognize that kind of mind-set? Have you ever been stuck because you just *had* to prove a point?

Jane was angry, but she was convinced there was nothing she *could* or *should* do about it. She had her ways, and changing them was of no interest to her. She had been fired from her job. Depressed and angry, she sat with her arms folded protectively over her heart, slumped in discouragement.

> Life is God's novel; let Him write it.
> —Isaac Singer

She whined, "I did not deserve to be fired. My life has never been fair. I've never had a chance. People always trip me up! I have to find another job, but when I do, the same things will happen all over again."

In truth, she had been fired from several jobs. When asked why, she said her reports were not in on time, she was "just a few minutes late" sometimes, she did not want to work overtime, and "oh, yeah," her supervisors said she was *sarcastic*. Big eye roll!

When her counselor asked her about the possibility of changing those actions in a future job, she became angry. She said her mother had abused her when she was a child. "She ruined my life, and I've never been successful at anything. No matter what I do, it won't do any good. Mother said I'd never please her or anybody else, and I never have!" And it was clear that she had made up her mind that she never would.

Jane had no intention of becoming successful. Her therapist asked, "If you become successful, what will happen?"

She disdainfully answered, "If I ever succeed at something, my mother will never realize how much she has hurt me. She would be off scot-free, just as she always is! That's *not* going to happen."

Jane had invested her life in showing her mother how damaged she was because of her mother's abuse. Her mother never owned up to the abuse she had inflicted, or asked for forgiveness for it, and Jane let a root of bitterness grow up in her life that nearly choked her to death. She had allowed her mother's words to become prophetic, destructive powers that controlled her life.

Jane had a choice to make. She could stick with her old story and keep holding her mother responsible for everything she had never accomplished, or she could write a new story.

Trying to Say Good-bye

You will recall that our friend Naomi was stuck in her old story too. She was a woman who recognized her plight but saw no hope for a new life. She was getting ready to leave Moab—the place of so many losses for her. If she had any idea God was waiting backstage to write her into a whole new drama, she gave no indication of it. She had told her daughters-in-law good-bye, and Orpah had left when we rejoin her on her way back to Bethlehem.

> Naomi said to Ruth, "Look, your sister-in-law is going back to her own people and her own gods. Go back with her."
>
> When Naomi saw that Ruth had firmly made up her mind to go with her, she stopped arguing with her. So Naomi

and Ruth went on until they came to the town of Bethlehem. When they entered Bethlehem, all the people became very excited. The women of the town said, "Is this really Naomi?"

Naomi answered the people, "Don't call me Naomi [pleasant]. Call me Mara [bitter], because the Almighty has made my life very sad. When I left, I had all I wanted, but now, the LORD has brought me home with nothing . . ."

So Naomi and her daughter-in-law Ruth, the Moabite, returned from Moab and arrived at Bethlehem at the beginning of the barley harvest. (vv. 15, 18–22)

Ah, the beginning of barley harvest. Little did Naomi know she was about to embark on something new. The same God who she believed had "made her life very sad" was just about to move in her life in ways she had never dreamed. After writing about years of bitterness, she was finally getting a new life. Barley harvest was here.

Who Will God Use in Your Story?

Chapter 2 of Ruth introduces a new character in Naomi's narrative. So often we do not know whom God will use to change the direction of our stories. That is one of those things we learn in retrospect in our own lives, but it is always interesting to see who has been a catalyst for change in another's life.

Read Ruth 2 and see how God introduces a hero, a man He will use to change the tenor and tone of Naomi's world. Interestingly, he had been there all along. He was not a knight who rode in on a white horse out of nowhere; he was her deceased husband's relative who had been in Bethlehem all along. His name was Boaz, and he was known as a "rich relative." That was just what Naomi needed at that point, a rich relative to take her in.

In the meantime Ruth decided she would go to the fields to gather some grain. Things were better but still pretty sparse for the two women. Ruth picked out a field where she could follow the gleaners and pick up the grain they dropped. And wouldn't you know, the field belonged to Boaz. When he inquired of his workers who she was, he was told she was "the young Moabite woman who came back with Naomi" (v. 6). The worker then described how diligently she had worked in the field, and Boaz was impressed with that report. Ruth had captured his attention. (Could it be that God had plans? Had He directed Boaz's gaze toward Ruth?) Boaz immediately spoke to Ruth, telling her to stay with his women workers to gather her grain, and she need not worry about the young men who were working in the field. They would not bother her, per his orders, and if she wanted water, it was freely available to her.

"Then Ruth bowed low with her face to the ground and said to him, 'I am not an Israelite. Why have you been so kind to notice me?'" (v. 10).

Notice her? He not only noticed her but also had her full résumé. She and Naomi had been the talk of Bethlehem when they returned. No doubt, Boaz had heard the town scuttlebutt and knew about all the help she had been to Naomi and the sacrifice she had made to come to a country that was not her own. He noticed all right, and he liked what he saw. In fact, he gave her a blessing. (This is one of my favorite "thank-you scriptures" I give to people who matter to me. It is rich. You might want to memorize it. It is Ruth 2:12.)

"May the LORD reward you for all you have done. May your wages be paid in full by the LORD, the God of Israel, under whose wings you have come for shelter."

Then Ruth said, "I hope I can continue to please you, sir. You have said kind and encouraging words to me, your servant, though I am not one of your servants."

Ah, sweet Ruth, please him? I think you already have pleased him beyond what you can imagine. Boaz invited her to join his people for a meal and then, when she went back to work, he told them to let her gather wherever she wanted to and to even drop a few heads of grain here and there to fatten her take for the day. Yes, I think she pleased him.

She went home to Naomi and told her all about her day. Don't you know that mother-in-law was glad to see her daughter-in-law come through the door?

> Ruth told her mother-in-law whose field she had worked in.
> She said, "The man I worked with today is named Boaz."
> Naomi told her daughter-in-law, "The LORD bless him! He continues to be kind to us—both the living and the dead!" Then Naomi told Ruth, "Boaz is one of our close relatives, one who should take care of us." (vv. 19–20)

So the plot thickens! Did you notice what Naomi said about Boaz? "Boaz is one of our close relatives, one who *should* take care of us." What was Boaz's obligation? Where was that command written? Let's look at two passages:

> If a person in your country becomes very poor and sells some land, then close relatives must come and buy it back. (Lev. 25:25)

If two brothers are living together, and one of them dies without having a son, his widow must not marry someone outside
her husband's family. Her husband's brother must marry her,
which is his duty to her as a brother-in-law. The first son she
has counts as the son of the dead brother so that his name will
not be forgotten in Israel. (Deut. 25:5–6)

What did Naomi know that Ruth did not know? The
"close relative," "nearest kinsman," or "kinsman redeemer"
in the Hebrew language is *goel*. The word means to "redeem,
receive, or buy back." The close relative had the responsibility
to keep the name and property of his deceased relative from
passing from the scene. If the deceased relative did not have an
heir, the closest male relative was obligated to marry the widowed woman and provide her with a child. It was a real act of
kindness because the firstborn son or any land he bought back
did not belong to him but to the relative who was deceased.
This seemed to be God's way of providing a new story for
those whose stories had come to tragic ends. Naomi had no
husband and no sons, but she had a close relative—a kinsman
redeemer—and she had Ruth.

Naomi's view of things was changing. Her old life was
becoming more and more a distant memory. Hope began to
dawn on the far horizon of her mind.

A New Story for Naomi

Naomi's new story emerges. She becomes quite the "arranger." It
is a very quaint picture of a powerful episode.

Then Naomi, Ruth's mother-in-law, said to her, "My daughter, I must find a suitable home for you, one that will be good for you. Now Boaz, whose young women you worked with, is our close relative. Tonight he will be working at the threshing floor. Wash yourself, put on perfume, change your clothes, and go down to the threshing floor. But don't let him know you're there until he has finished his dinner. Watch him so you will know where he lies down to sleep. When he lies down, go and lift the cover off his feet and lie down. He will tell you what you should do." (3:1–4)

These were peculiar directions, granted, but Ruth trusted Naomi. She recognized that she was herself a Moabite, and there were things she did not know about the customs in Naomi's land. If she was going to live the new life she had chosen when she followed Naomi, she knew she would need to follow her instructions implicitly, which she did. And sure enough, after supper she looked around for Boaz and quickly found him asleep by a pile of grain.

Ruth went to him quietly and lifted the cover from his feet and lay down.

About midnight Boaz was startled and rolled over. There was a woman lying near his feet! Boaz asked, "Who are you?"

She said, "I am Ruth, your servant girl. Spread your cover over me, because you are a relative who is supposed to take care of me."

Then Boaz said, "The LORD bless you, my daughter. This act of kindness is greater than the kindness you showed to Naomi in the beginning. You didn't look for a young man to marry, either rich or poor . . . It is true that I am a relative who is to take care of you, but you have a closer relative than I." (vv. 7–10, 12)

Uh-oh. This could be a complication in Naomi's plan. She had plotted out a new story for Ruth and potentially for herself, but there was a *closer* relative. What would he do? Another twist in the plot, just like a great mystery novel. What would happen next? Ruth had virtually *asked* Boaz to marry her by lying at his feet. That is not our custom today, but you can imagine the picture: a surprised Boaz and a humble Ruth on the threshing floor in the middle of the night. Her actions were deliberate and obedient. The results were not in her hands.

We only can do so much to write a new story, but we at least need to take the steps we know to take. Once that is done, we wait and leave the rest to God.

Boaz says, commenting on the closer relative,

Stay here tonight, and in the morning we will see if he will take care of you. If he decides to take care of you, that is fine. But if he refuses, I will take care of you myself, as surely as the LORD lives. So stay here until morning. (v. 13)

So Ruth stayed at his feet until morning, but it was not yet daylight when he asked her to spread out her shawl. He filled it with six portions of barley and sent her on her way.

So Ruth returned to Naomi, who was anxiously waiting for a report. She gave her a full rundown of the night, including the fact that Boaz had sent Naomi a gift of six portions of barley.

Naomi saw everything that happened as a good sign that Boaz would take care of everything. She was so confident that she told Ruth just to wait and see what would happen.

New stories often involve "wait and see." Ruth was really walking in blind faith. She trusted Naomi and committed herself to follow her. That was what she knew about her new story, but Naomi put her on alert to wait for more, and she would see!

The Transaction

The story becomes intriguing and finally resolves in Chapter 4 as God makes the story He planned to write work out for good. Look for the backstory that had been there all along. Examine the character of Boaz. What did he have that Naomi and Ruth needed so they could write their new stories? Watch how he handles what could have been a delicate situation.

> Boaz went to the city gate and sat there until the close relative he had mentioned passed by. Boaz called to him, "Come here, friend, and sit down." So the man came over and sat down. Boaz gathered ten of the elders of the city and told them, "Sit down here!" So they sat down. (4:1–2)

And the negotiations began. Boaz explained Naomi's plight to the closer relative. He then offered him the opportunity to buy Naomi's land, since he was the next in line to do so. The man jumped on the idea! "I'll buy it."

Then Boaz said, "There is one more thing to consider. If you buy the land, you will have to marry Ruth, the Moabite widow."

The close relative said, "No deal. If I do that, I could mess

up the inheritance I plan to give to my sons. You buy the land."
Then he did something unusual to seal the deal.

Long ago in Israel when people traded or bought back something, one person took off his sandal and gave it to the other person. This was the proof of ownership in Israel.

So the close relative said to Boaz, "Buy the land yourself," and he took off his sandal.

> Then Boaz said to the elders and to all the people, "You are witnesses today. I am buying from Naomi everything that belonged to Elimelech and Kilion and Mahlon. I am also taking Ruth, the Moabite who was the wife of Mahlon, as my wife. I am doing this so her dead husband's property will stay in his name and his name will not be separated from his family and his hometown. You are witnesses today." (vv. 9–10)

It was official. Naomi's story had changed. Ruth's story had changed. Boaz's story had changed. Each of them was living the same life as before, but in the midst of all the pain and sadness of the women's history, God propelled them to new futures; futures of redemption, new life, and great purpose. In addition, these three would soon witness the miracle of new life.

> So Boaz took Ruth home as his wife and had sexual relations with her. The LORD let her become pregnant, and she gave birth to a son. The women told Naomi, "Praise the LORD who gave you this grandson. May he become famous in Israel. He will give you new life and will take care of you in your old age because of your daughter-in-law who loves

you. She is better for you than seven sons, because she has given birth to your grandson." (vv. 13-15)

Naomi took the boy, held him in her arms, and cared for him. The neighbors gave the boy his name, saying, "This boy was born for Naomi." They named him Obed. Obed was the father of Jesse, and Jesse was the father of David (v. 17).

David. That's King David! Naomi's old role as a lonely, distraught widow had changed to her new identity as great-great-grandmother to the greatest king in the history of Israel. Oh yes, it is possible to write a new story!

Take the Plunge

As you reflect on this chapter, can you find three nuggets to save in your treasure chest of wise words? This kind of treasure chest can hold truths that make you stronger in the days ahead. If you are delaying the writing of your new story, go ahead and take the plunge! If God has been prompting you about some action you need to take, why not say yes and begin? Or maybe you know there is an attitude holding you back. Maybe you have a lack of forgiveness or an exasperation keeping you stuck. God has ways of healing those parts of us that we are willing to turn over to Him. He will work in the places that only He can work and leave the choices He wants us to make in our hands.

Is it time for you to pick up your pen or sit down at your computer? Is it time to bow your head and pray, "God, help"? God promises that He is listening. He hears the whispers of your heart.

Personal Reflection

1. What three nuggets of wisdom did you find in this chapter?
2. What lessons can you apply to your own life from Naomi's story?
3. A friend of mine sometimes says she feels so low she has to "look up to see the bottom." Have you ever been at the total bottom of life? Describe that time and how it made you feel.
4. Do you see yourself there now, or is it just a memory?
5. Can you see how you might begin to write a new story?
6. Do you want to write a new story but can't figure out where to begin?
7. Has anyone encouraged you to begin again? What did you hear them say to you? How have you responded to them up until now?
8. After studying Naomi's story, how would you respond to them now?

Journal Entry

To begin your new story, complete the following starter sentence in your personal journal. Then continue writing thoughts and feelings from your heart as long as you need to.

I know the time has come in my life for me to leave my old story behind and begin a new one because . . .

Group Discussion Questions

1. Why do you think it's so difficult to leave our "old stories" behind? And why is beginning again a scary and hard thing to face even when our old stories are bad ones? (Example: Statistics show that an abused woman who finally escapes from her abusive husband often ends up going back to her abusive situation. Why do you think that's true?)

2. What courageous step did Naomi take to begin her new story?

3. What do you think would have happened to Naomi and Ruth if they had stayed in Moab?

4. You've heard the old adage, "When God closes a door, He always opens a window." Do you believe that's true? Explain.

5. When God opens a window or new door, does He ever have to *push us* through it to our new beginnings? Explain.

6. How did Ruth's loyalty and obedience to Naomi lead to a new story for her?

7. Give an example of a time when God offered you a new story and how you responded.

Chapter 2

DON'T BE
HELD HOSTAGE
BY THE PAST

*Any change, even a change for the better, is always
accompanied by drawbacks and discomforts.*

—Arnold Bennett

Leah

Leah changed her theme in the midst of
a humiliating situation.

GENESIS 29:16—30:21

Leah had an unhappy life—there's no question about it. First, she was evidently not really a pretty woman because her eyes were weak. So the men in their circle passed over her as a potential wife. To make it even worse, she had a younger sister named Rachel who was gorgeous, sweet, and probably very popular with the men they knew. Living in her family was not fun for Leah.

Then along comes Jacob in search of a wife. He falls in love with Rachel at first sight, overlooking Leah. And after working for the girl's father for seven long years to earn Rachel as his wife, Jacob is deceived by him, and Leah is substituted for Rachel at the wedding. She is foisted off on Jacob, who did not want her. Worse yet, Jacob also gets to marry his great love, Rachel, so Leah ends up as the third wheel in a loveless marriage.

It is no surprise that Leah's attitude or story is not one of gratitude and joy. But when God gets involved, the plot of Leah's story takes an astonishing turn.

My daddy was a funny, devoted, hardworking man, who totally loved his only child. When I was getting ready to leave for college, he took time to have a talk with me. We had been running an errand in the old red Plymouth Fury. (I always loved that car.) When we pulled into the driveway, he turned off the motor and said, "Boose" (my nickname left over from "beautiful baby"), "I don't care how far you go away or what you ever do, you can always come home."

That was all he wanted to say, but that was enough. I believed it. I knew he had my back, and no matter what, he was there for me.

I carried this message with me through four years of college and many years of adult life. I knew I could always go home. I never had to, but I knew my daddy had the door propped open, just in case. That was one of the reasons it was so sad to me when I began to see changes in him—changes that were so uncharacteristic. He became antagonistic, confused, and difficult to handle. My mother, who was the love of his life, became the object of his antagonism, and it was not long before I, his only child, was in the same place.

Mother and I were stunned. Who was this man? What had happened? We did not know it at the time, but creeping dementia was stealing him away. We trudged through the next years with the ups and downs of daily dramas that create a surreal story around those afflicted by this debilitating disease. We did not have a clue what this story would bring or how it would end. We took each day as it came, praying that we would know what to do next. We knew we could not continue to care for him at home, but we also could not bear the thought of *not* doing it. At last, God intervened in our dilemma. As I sat by his bed one late afternoon, he quietly shivered and began to breathe erratically. Within a couple of hours, he died.

That awful, frightening chapter in our story had finally come to an end. Our hearts were broken, our energy sapped. There had been no redemption. The only way out had been death. It hurt and was so wrong, but we could either continue to carry that hard backstory around or begin a new story.

After several more months of grieving (there had already been so much), Mother began to look forward. Within the year, like Naomi, she moved back to her childhood hometown and began again in a retirement apartment. She lived another twelve years. During those days, we often laughed about things Daddy had said in the old days. We fondly remembered trips we had made, pets they had shared, and the doting love he lavished on his grandsons.

We never again rehearsed the scenes of the dementia years, although that story was not forgotten. We could not forget, but there was no point in dragging it into the rest of our lives. There was no good reason to relive the scenes that had torn us apart. The good memories survived and warmed my mother's heart until she went to her grave, and the good memories stay with me today.

Writing a new story in your life does not mean you never think of the past. You do not just forget what you have lived through. You become the sum total of your life experiences, so you really cannot move into selective amnesia. You cannot build a new playbook for your life without the influence of yesterday. We *are* who we *are*, and we come from where we come from. That's a fact. There is, however, that moment of awakening when you realize you have more power than you thought. You have the power to change how you react to life. You do not have to be controlled by where you come from or by what happened to you. When you realize that, you open doors for *wanted* change, or at the very least, *needed* change. You cannot choose what happens to you, but you can choose how you respond to it. It is all about attitude.

Repeating Themes

Some deadly beliefs can undermine your having a good attitude. In his book *What Happy People Know*, Dr. Dan Baker sums them up as well and as simply as I have ever seen them stated. Have you ever heard any of these thoughts going through your mind?

- I've been victimized.
- I'm entitled to more.
- I'll be rescued.
- Someone else is to blame.[1]

Repeated themes like these can be overwhelming to healthy thinking. Victimization has many degrees and comes from various sources. Some are more affected than others. The reality is, however, that we all have been victimized in one way or another.

Then we are quickly led to believe we deserve more, someone else needs to help us out of the mess, and we have to blame someone. It is all a package that has the consistent theme "I am stuck because I'm a victim." Yet you are the only one who can break the cycle of circular thinking that goes nowhere.

You have to start by declaring the truth, "Someone may have hurt me, but I am not a victim. God has given me what I need. I may think I deserve more, but until He gives me more, I will be content with His choice. He will rescue me in His time. And there is no value in blaming someone else." That truth must be mentally rehearsed, perhaps many times. Then you will begin to see your theme gradually change. Asking yourself some simple questions will help you get to the truth, if you will take the time to really think them through. Here is a good place to begin.

What theme from my childhood am I still carrying? Rudolf Dreikurs, the psychiatrist, once said, "Children are keen observers, but poor interpreters." I have found this to be true. Many people live their lives according to what they *think* they know because they learned to believe it in childhood.

This happened to a little girl named Josie. A favorite uncle brought her a puppy. Josie and her uncle happily sat on the front porch and played with the puppy. When the uncle got up to go inside, he was unaware the puppy had followed him through the heavy front door. Sadly, the door swung shut and broke the puppy's neck as Josie watched.

Josie was heartbroken over her puppy. At the same time, she developed a strong dislike for the man who had been her favorite uncle. In fact, until she was a teenager, she avoided him as much as possible. She appeared to be genuinely afraid of him and would not speak about or to him at all. Years later Josie's father questioned her one more time about her dislike of her uncle.

Josie said, "He gave me a puppy. Then he let the door slam and kill him." Josie's interpretation of the facts was accurate, but as a child, she did not have the ability to see the total picture—that it was an accident.

Think of the children you know. How well do they interpret what happens to them? When trauma or sadness is experienced in childhood, we do not have the maturity to see the whole picture. At that time in our lives, we only know what we can see so we begin to build a life on what we *thought* was totally true. It is easy for an event of childhood to hold us hostage until we stop, look back, and try to see the truth. This is more common than any of us might imagine and why writing a new story often requires a clear-eyed inspection of what we believe and why.

"Children are keen observers, but poor interpreters."

A friend of mine, who works with women, told me about a woman she knew who was afraid of bridges. When she was five years old, an old wooden bridge gave way under the weight of the car in which she was riding with her mother. Their car fell into the river, but they were rescued. When the woman became a teenager and got her driver's license, she panicked when she had to drive across a bridge. When asked what she was afraid of, the young woman said matter-of-factly, "Bridges break and people drown." She had made a lifetime belief from one childhood experience.

The only way she could write a new story was to begin driving over bridges that appeared to be safe. She began with short bridges, and gradually she became able to drive over longer ones. Her childhood belief had to be challenged and replaced. When you are stuck in the middle of an irrational story, but it feels much too hard to write a new one, try to track down the source of your belief. You will probably find some sort of childhood connection. When I say *childhood*, that extends to the teen years and young twenties as well. They all are formative years in our lives.

Fact or Feelings?

Leigh is a woman who went through a really rough time during her teenage years. Her parents divorced. Her father remarried, and her mom began life as a single parent. Leigh was torn between the two of them. Instead of believing she still had a life with both of them and was wanted by both of them, she convinced herself they had both rejected her. This gave everything that happened to her in her twenties and thirties an interesting spin. She learned to interpret certain phrases and actions as rejection. Several relationships fell apart in her life because she interpreted innocent behaviors as slights. She disliked herself for pushing back at the perceived rejections in her life. She was often surprised by her own reactions.

When Leigh was forty, her husband, Tim, asked her to go to counseling with him. He was a mild-mannered guy who loved Leigh dearly, but he found himself stepping on her emotional land mines more frequently than he wanted. He could not convince her that he was not rejecting her. No matter what he said or did, she read it as a slight, an offense, or a rejection. She interpreted his words and actions just as she had her father's. "He doesn't care. He doesn't even know what matters to me. He doesn't see me." Clearly, this had become a real problem between them. Tim had no defense. She could only see what he said and did through her eyes.

Leigh's childhood interpretation of her parents' actions had made her act like a marionette on a string. She did well until some perceived rejection tangled her strings, then she was stuck. A wise counselor helped Leigh see that she was being controlled. Her perceptions were working against her, determining her responses; she was not seeing the truth of what was really happening.

Leigh discovered that, in order to untangle herself, she had to be aware of the beginning feelings of rejection that came over her when she *perceived* rejection. She learned to recognize that the familiar, irritating sensation she felt was the same feeling she had when she tried to talk to her dad after the divorce. She felt dismissed, and it enraged her. Her twisted interpretation of how things were kicked in when those feelings began. That is what happens to us sometimes. *Feelings* capture our attention while the *facts* lie dormant in our thinking.

Leigh had to learn to challenge her own feelings. No one else could challenge her because the feeling rendered her unreasonable. The counselor helped her learn to talk herself out of it by speaking the truth in her head. "Tim is *not* my father and he is not rejecting me," or "Just because Rosa is disagreeing with me, it doesn't mean she doesn't want to be my friend." It was not easy, but it was effective.

Leigh's real success came when she looked back at what had happened in her life and how she had learned to interpret it. She realized the grid through which she saw life had been skewed when her world had been so thrown off kilter by her parents' divorce. The pain of it all had short-circuited her ability to see things as they really are in some specific areas, particularly when it came to whether or not she was acceptable. That is a tough place to feel insecure.

A Woman Named *Cow*

In the Scriptures we meet a woman who surely had to reason with herself about her value, her place in the family, and her position in her husband's heart. Just to give you a sense of what she was up against, imagine if your name meant "cow" and your sister's name meant "ewe." Right there you could have some issues.

The "cow" in this case was Leah, and the "ewe," or "little lamb," was her sister, Rachel. The Scriptures describe them this way: "Now Laban had two daughters: the name of the elder was Leah, and the name of the younger was Rachel. Leah's eyes were delicate [weak], but Rachel was beautiful of form and appearance" (Gen. 29:16–17 NKJV, brackets mine).

It is interesting that the Scriptures stop with Leah's eyes. Was there nothing else about which to comment? Was she only known as "Cow with delicate eyes"? The consensus could be that "Cow" lacked many of the beautiful qualities of her sister, "Ewe." Reality check: those facts were not going to change.

For all of us there are certain unchanging truths. Some parts of our stories we can alter with different thinking and behavior, but our looks are typically our looks. God made us what we are physically, and that is one of the first issues of interpretation we have to deal with as we grow up. What is *is*, and you have to ask yourself, *Can I accept that?*

The family into which we are born is another what-if. We can pine away for what might have been, but our looks and our family line are pretty well set in stone. (I understand the exceptions of plastic surgery and adoption, but the original package is what we find in most of our stories, and the subconscious influence is there.)

So Leah and Rachel were sisters in a family that included their wily father, Laban, who was a case study himself. No doubt his daughters had to deal with his ways from the time they were very young. We can see how he related to each of them in the story we read in Genesis 29, but before we get there, I will give you a little of the backstory so you can see the bigger picture. Take some time and get to know these sisters, their father, and the man they *both* will marry. Put yourself in each of their places and ask yourself what your struggle would have been. This is the kind of tale that makes for incredible drama. Romance entwined with treachery always sells!

Every Life Has Themes

Life stories always seem to have themes. They come from the words we have heard and believed and the words we continually repeat to ourselves. You may not know you have themes in your life, or you may have some that are dormant but still affect you. This might be a good time to poke around in your thinking and see if you know your themes, good or bad. Do you find yourself anywhere in the following?

- If you can't do it perfectly, then don't do it at all.
- It costs too much.
- If you have to ask how much it costs, you can't afford it.

- Always check the right side of the menu; price is most important.
- I never learned how to handle money.
- Drama, drama, drama—there's always drama.
- That's just the way I am.
- I am sick.
- Why does this always happen to me?
- What have I done to deserve this?
- Someone always gets the prize before I do.
- No is not an answer.
- You just have to take what comes.
- That's the hand you were dealt.
- You never know.
- If it's not one thing, it's another.
- It's always something.
- I know because I know, and I always know.
- What does God want from me?
- I've made my bed, now I have to lie in it.
- I have to do it, or it won't get done.
- Fill in the blank with your theme:

  _____.

When it occurs to you that you are living in a story that has a theme without hope of change, that is an awakening. You may want to go back to sleep because you do not want to face the day. But recognizing you are not stuck and you do not have to keep thinking and doing the same things is an essential first step to writing a new story—to getting a life. Sticking to your old ways, insisting that you cannot live another way, will leave you paralyzed. Recognizing that something has to change is a harbinger of hope!

The best place to focus is on what is working and what is not. If the theme you have relied on to be true for so much of your life is not working for you, then it is probably a good time to change it. Even if you think it is a pretty good credo, you may want to look at the people around you to see how they are responding. Do they buy what you think is true and rely on that to be your theme, or do they roll their eyes and seem to say, "That's just the way she is, and she is not going to change"?

If that is the case, then it is probably pretty clear that you are stuck in your backstory. You are reliving old scenes and clinging to old themes that are keeping you bound in what seemed right, or they're keeping you in the humdrum of an unlived life.

Repeating the Same Theme Can Grow Old

I have met women in grief who repeatedly tell a story of sadness and loss. Of course, that is to be expected at first because the pain is so deep and hard to bear. It must be repeated over and over for healing to even begin. It cannot be bottled up and only rehearsed internally. That is part of the process, and for some who believe letting go of the story is letting go of a connection with their loved ones, it takes a longer time.

The realization that rehashing the story does not bring the loved ones back or keep them connected often brings a new day. That is the day grieving people wake up and are somehow strangely tired of telling the old story. It does not make their loss any less, but they no longer want to continue dragging around their old worn-out stories of pain and sadness like a ball on a chain. That is the day a new story can begin. The old story is still there, but a new story is starting. The strong themes of the past cannot be continuously repeated in the new.

My friend Michelle lost her young husband after five years of battling brain cancer. He had been the picture of health and virility when she met and married him, but within a few weeks, his unbearable headaches cast them into a story over which they had no control. Surgery, chemotherapy, altered brain function, and the inevitability of dying pulled them along while they tried to make some sense out of the life they were living. They were not strangers to the overarching love and power of God, so they fervently clung to the hope that some way, somehow, God would intervene in their unbelievable circumstances and show Himself to be the mighty healer.

In the meantime, they prayed, waited, and immersed themselves in the grueling, painful process of trying to beat the odds. Life was nothing like they wanted, but they truly believed God would show Himself as powerful, no matter what the outcome. Halfway through their fight, their story took a dramatic turn— God did intervene. He did not heal, but He gave new life. For one short period of time during the treatment process, there was a three-month window when conceiving a child was possible. Not knowing what the future held, or whether they could actually have a baby, they left the story to God. He graciously gave them a wonderful child that his daddy got to know for two and a half years.

Greg's earthly story ended five years after it took the violent turn into the world of cancer and the fight for survival. He wrote a valiant saga, but the ending was God's to tell. On a quiet September morning, Greg died in the house he and Michelle had bought as their first home. Michelle and young Clay lived on to write a new story they were not seeking, but one God clearly had planned for them long before Michelle knew she would be widowed and her son would be fatherless. In the aftermath of Greg's death, the grief lingered with Michelle. It had been with her like a seeping wound for the five years of Greg's illness. She had been drained of dreams, and her focus became giving Clay the life and the parenting he deserved.

Michelle had determined early on, however, that she was not going to live the rest of her days identified as Greg's widow. In her maturing heart she seemed to know that holding on to grief and the old story would lock her into an identity she did not want to bear throughout her life. Although Greg's illness and death had been an incredibly difficult blow, she knew God was still God and that if she were still alive, He had a story for her to live.

Enter Bryan, a young widower whose wife had died of cancer five years before. His story was the sad and difficult story of a father left with two children to rear without his wife and their mother. He, too, knew that God was bigger than all of his pain and suffering, but he did not know how to move forward. How could he make the grief subside in order to move into the new life God had for him?

Grief brings a lot of questions into the picture. The themes of loss and faint hope seem to ripple through the chapters of each day as mental ponderings: *How will I get through this? How will my heart heal? How will I find a new "normal"? Do I even want to find a new "normal"? What about the memories? I don't want to forget the one I loved. I don't want the children to forget their mother or daddy.* These are all issues associated with grief that put their stamps on every page of life.

When we remember that God knows our grief and is acquainted with our sorrows, many times it is a matter of letting time take us to the next intersection, to the next character or plot He has planned for us. If we will not be tightly bound to the old story, the new story can begin to emerge, and we can find the next chapters that are waiting to be written.

Unfortunately, some of us delay the next chapters by holding on to the past too tightly. We do not want to move on. We do not want to leave our past worlds or the people in them. We resist the very idea of new stories, so we often find ourselves stuck in grief and our own miserable pain.

Michelle and Bryan turned their faces toward the future when they met. Slowly at first, but with a steady view toward a potential new story, they got acquainted, determined they wanted to move on together, and were married. Michelle became mother to two preteens, and Bryan gained an elementary-age son. They were both living the same life, but they were launching a new story together.

> God . . . writes with a soft-tipped pen when He deals with our broken and grieving hearts.

This new story would have been impossible if they had individually clung to grief and refused to allow their hurts to be healed out of loyalty to their first mates. It would have been impossible if they had maintained their mourning and refused to see that "weeping may last for the night, but a shout of joy comes in the morning" (Ps. 30:5 NASB).

Neither they nor their children will be able to change their original stories. Those stories will always be part of who they are and where they came from. Still, they can allow God to propel them forward, knowing He writes with a soft-tipped pen when He deals with our broken and grieving hearts.

Maybe you struggle with grief. Perhaps you hate the loss but long for a new story. You may allow fear to make you hesitant and timid about moving forward, but you will know when the day to move on has come. It is the day you are tired of hearing your old story retold. It is the day you feel a longing for fresh air and new life. You will hear yourself telling the old story, but it will not hold the same interest or connection for you as it once did. Grief has done her work when you can move on in your thoughts and conversation—the revealing actions of your heart.

Ages

It is easy to get stuck in a certain way of thinking as you arrive at particular ages. Now that I am beyond it, I never cease to be amazed at the women who live under the perpetual domination of menopause. It is as if arriving at that age welded them into the eternal hot-flashing, forever-cranky woman. I always want to say to them, "You will survive, and there *is* life after the change." For many women in their forties and fifties, a new story would be glorious. Menopause happens and life goes on! Being middle-aged is not the end of the world. In fact, it is a bridge from where you were to a whole other life free of all of the perils of fertility!

Then there is old age. I had a birthday not too long ago. I smiled to myself and rolled my eyes a little when I bought an airline ticket online and had to identify myself as a "senior." The day before I was part of the general population, but my birthday kicked me into the category of the oldest citizens flying. For some reason that had to go on my airline profile. Since I am now a Medicare card-carrying senior citizen, and flying as an elder on the airline, I have to determine what story I will tell. I do not want to be the typical old lady. I do not mind being old, but I really do not want to live the stereotypical life of what my daddy used to call "the blue hairs." They were elderly women who had a rinse put on their hair to enhance their gray, and it left a blue tinge until it wore off a bit! I am choosing to "get a life," even if my profile says, "You're old."

Many times new stories come from the in-spite-ofs rather than the because-ofs.

I have a friend who is "old" like I am, who plans to start working on her PhD this year—the year of her sixty-fifth birthday. People have asked her if she knows how old she will be when she gets her doctorate. She answers, "The same age I would be if I didn't know how old I was." She is not allowing age to dictate what she does. She is going after her advanced degree, not because of her age, but in spite of it. Many times new stories come from the in-spite-ofs rather than the because-ofs.

Stages

Pregnancy, empty nest, retirement, divorce, or job loss are all transitional stages of life. They present opportunities to create a new story. In fact, these stages will almost *propel* you into a new story. It is hard to hang on to the old story in these circumstances without rehashing a lot of life that has passed you by. Old stories can be good to repeat occasionally, but if new stages are not embraced, old stories can become your signature, and you will find yourself slowed down or stopped. Stagnated stages will cause you to look back and serve as a great breeding ground for stunted thinking.

A new perspective often requires a new story. If you see things in a different way, it will change the way you relate to the world. If your child has a baby when she is single, facing all the problems that come with that scenario, it will change *your* story. You will probably become an advocate for young women who become single parents, although you have had a mate all of your adult life. Perspective influences everything.

One of my friends had always drawn a very clear line in the sand in her thinking about divorce. She staunchly stood on "no, no, no," until her daughter married an abusive man who defied every norm my friend had ever known. Her daughter was trapped and terrified, thousands of miles away from home. My friend's old story did not play out so well then. She became very interested in looking at the divorce issue with totally new eyes. Her hard-lined, black-and-white view began to take on softer shades of gray. She developed a new perspective, her daughter was rescued, and they both have a new way of seeing things today. Perspective is everything.

A Biblical Soap Opera

Changing scenes and themes can seem like an overwhelming task, especially when we find ourselves ensnared by circumstances beyond our control. Remember Leah? It is hard to imagine any woman being dealt a poorer hand than Leah. Remember that her daddy, Laban, named her Cow? Leah also became a pawn in a complex game between two men, eventually landing her in a loveless marriage. She became a co-wife with her beautiful baby sister, Rachel, that sweet little Ewe in her daddy's eyes. Talk about a soap opera!

The man who would show up at Leah's doorstep was named

Jacob, meaning "one who supplants." (A *supplanter* takes advantage of others by underhanded tactics.) He was about to meet his match in Uncle Laban. Leah's world was soon to change, and Rachel would find that she had limitations she never imagined. Remember, she was always "the loved one." Things had always gone well in her story, unlike her older sister, Leah. Take a look at Leah's story in Genesis 29 and see how she changed her theme in the midst of a terrible situation.

Jacob has come to his Uncle Laban's territory to escape from the wrath of his brother, Esau, whom he had conned out of his birthright. Esau vowed to kill him and their mother, so Rebekah sent Jacob to stay with her brother, Laban. Eventually he arrived and found the well where Laban watered his sheep. "While Jacob was talking with the shepherds, Rachel came with her father's sheep, because it was her job to care for the sheep. . . . Then Jacob kissed Rachel and cried. He told her that he was from her father's family and that he was the son of Rebekah. So Rachel ran home and told her father" (vv. 9, 11–12). Laban was delighted to see Jacob and said to him, "You are my own flesh and blood" (v. 14).

The Trickster Is Tricked

Now we will see how Jacob, the trickster who had fooled his father and brother, was himself tricked into a life he did not want. The plot takes another unwelcome twist!

> Jacob stayed there a month. Then Laban said to Jacob, "You are my relative, but it is not right for you to work for me without pay. What would you like me to pay you?"

Now Laban had two daughters. The older was Leah, and the younger was Rachel. Leah had weak eyes, but Rachel was very beautiful. Jacob loved Rachel, so he said to Laban, "Let me marry your younger daughter Rachel. If you will, I will work seven years for you."

Laban said, "It would be better for her to marry you than someone else, so stay here with me." So Jacob worked for Laban seven years so he could marry Rachel. But they seemed like just a few days to him because he loved Rachel very much. (vv. 15–20)

Now, let's see how Jacob's hard work eventually paid off:

After seven years Jacob said to Laban, "Give me Rachel so that I may marry her. The time I promised to work for you is over."

So Laban gave a feast for all the people there. That evening he brought his daughter Leah to Jacob, and they had sexual relations. (Laban gave his slave girl Zilpah to his daughter to be her servant.) In the morning when Jacob saw that he had had sexual relations with Leah, he said to Laban, "What have you done to me? I worked hard for you so that I could marry Rachel! Why did you trick me?"

Laban said, "In our country we do not allow the younger daughter to marry before the older daughter. But complete the full week of the marriage ceremony with Leah, and I will give you Rachel to marry also. But you must serve me another seven years."

So Jacob did this, and when he had completed the week with Leah, Laban gave him his daughter Rachel as a wife. (Laban gave his slave girl Bilhah to his daughter Rachel to be her servant.) So Jacob had sexual relations with Rachel also, and Jacob loved Rachel more than Leah. Jacob worked for Laban for another seven years. (vv. 21–30)

What a shock! Think about it: You work seven long, hard years in the desert heat with smelly sheep for the woman you love, based on an agreement with your father-in-law-to-be. Then, on your wedding night, you end up with her sister! Not only that, but then you are also told you can still have the one you love, *but* you will need to work seven *more* years in the desert heat with smelly sheep for her. Is anyone just a little surprised that Jacob was slightly more than ticked off at such an incredible deception? And this was no temporary arrangement—it was marriage! It was forever. This old story would just keep on going it seemed, for both Jacob and Leah. What possible new story could emerge?

God's Mercy

In His great mercy, God noticed Leah's plight and took pity on her. Let's see what He did for her.

> When the LORD saw that Jacob loved Rachel more than Leah, he made it possible for Leah to have children, but not Rachel. Leah became pregnant and gave birth to a son. She named him Reuben, because she said, "The LORD has seen my troubles. Surely now my husband will love me."
>
> Leah became pregnant again and gave birth to another son. She named him Simeon and said, "The LORD has heard that I am not loved, so he has given me this son."

Leah became pregnant again and gave birth to another son. She named him Levi and said, "Now, surely my husband will be close to me, because I have given him three sons."

Then Leah gave birth to another son. She named him Judah, because she said, "Now I will praise the LORD." Then Leah stopped having children. (vv. 31–35)

After years of suffering the disdain of her husband, even though she bore him four sons, Leah turned to a new page in her story. She evidently grew tired of her old story of self-pity and realized how blessed by God she truly was in spite of the other difficulties in her marriage and life. Then her song of pity turned into a song of praise and her new story began on a high note.

The interesting long-term outcome of Leah's new attitude and story is that her fourth son, Judah—the son of her song of praise—became the father of the most important tribe in all of Israel. It was through his tribe that God sent His only Son into the world. And Jesus, the Christ, the Savior of the world, became known as the "Lion of Judah." Now that's what you call a great ending to a story!

Personal Reflection

1. Leah's story shows us there is never a situation so bad that we cannot choose to think a new way. Describe a difficult circumstance in your life that has caused you to become stuck in an old way of thinking.

2. How do you think Leah felt about herself in comparison to Rachel?

3. Do you struggle with how you look or feel about yourself? Describe that struggle.

4. Have you ever wondered why you were born into your family of origin or why your childhood was as it was? Explain.

5. What theme do you see in your life? Briefly trace that theme through the events of your life.

6. Do you want to continue living that theme, or do you want to change it? Explain.

7. If you change the theme of your life, what do you want the new theme to become?

8. How can you use Leah's example to change how you think about your situation?

Journal Entry

To continue your new story, complete the following starter sentence in your personal journal. Then continue writing thoughts and feelings from your heart as long as you need to.

I would like to change the theme of my life because . . .

Group Discussion Questions

1. What do we learn from the Bible text (Gen. 29) about the differences in Leah and Rachel?

2. Which sister does Jacob love the most and why?

3. At what agreement do Jacob and Laban arrive? Would you have trusted either of them, knowing what you know about the family from which they both came?

4. Do you think Jacob had a déjà vu experience when Laban tricked him? Why? Read Genesis 27 to get a deeper understanding of Jacob's story and the reason for his possible déjà vu.

5. How long will the consequences of Laban's deception last?

6. What does Leah name her first three sons and why? Who is the focus in each of the names?

7. What does Leah name her fourth child, and what does she say about him? Where is her focus placed in naming him?

8. What themes do you hear in Leah's old story?

9. How do you see Leah's thinking change in the midst of her loveless marriage?

10. What new theme do you think Leah was weaving into her life?

11. What lessons can we learn from Leah's new story?

Chapter 3

ASK YOURSELF THE GOOD QUESTIONS ONLY YOU CAN ASK

The most erroneous stories are those we think we know best—and therefore never scrutinize or question.

—Stephen Jay Gould

Rahab

Rahab saved her family and her own
neck as a result of acting on the truth.

JOSHUA 2–6

Rahab was a harlot. A prostitute. A madam who operated a
"guest house" in the city of Jericho. She was well known as one of
the "bad women" in town. Everyone in Jericho knew her for what
she was. She was not accepted in the prestigious social circles of
the city. Rather, she was likely shunned and ignored by *decent*
people. So she knew her place.

Then one day two of God's special spies showed up at
Rahab's door, and she took them in. They were there to spy out
the city before God's people captured it. If Rahab got caught
with them in her house, the king would surely punish her or,
perhaps, even kill her.

Why would a prostitute help godly men anyway? The two
do not seem to go together, do they? And yet that is exactly what
Rahab did. She hid the spies from the king of Jericho's men and
helped them escape into the mountains. She changed her way of
thinking, and as a result, she received an unusual promise from
God about a red rope and was able to begin a new story that had
a truly surprising conclusion.

Believing you are doing the right thing can be a trap if you do not learn to ask yourself good questions. Failure to consider what the outcome of your thinking and behavior will be can put you in the middle of a story you do not want to tell.

My friend Katherine allowed herself to be drawn into a story where another person wrote the script, and it almost destroyed her life. Katherine and Jen became friends at work. They ate lunch together, took their breaks together, and soon became enmeshed in one another's lives. Katherine was clueless that another person could take control of her emotions to the point that she could lose all sense of what was appropriate or right; consequently, she was swept away before she knew it. I saw it happen.

The once bubbly, vivacious, deal-with-anything woman became secretive, morose, and evasive. After the fact, I learned that she felt sorry for Jen and tried to befriend her in ways that would make her life better. The closer they became, the more needy Jen seemed to be. She often complained about her husband's lack of empathy, so it only seemed right for Katherine to give it to her.

Little by little, Jen moved into Katherine's emotions, and Katherine found that her life was being taken over. The people who really mattered to her were finding fewer roles to play in her story. Jen was taking all of her attention and much of her time.

Katherine had no idea that the connection she and Jen had was really a set of hooks deep in her emotions. When Jen felt bad, Katherine felt bad. When Jen was upset, Katherine was upset. If Jen needed her, Katherine dropped everything and went to her side. The quirky thing was that the more Jen said about her husband's lack of empathy, the more Katherine's husband seemed to fall short too. She grew to resent him and turned all her emotions toward Jen. That suited Jen just fine. It filled the void she had had for many years.

Katherine never stopped to question if this was the way she wanted her story to read. She never paused to ask herself if this connection was good or destructive. She just never asked herself any questions. As a result, she sunk into a deep pit of involvement before it began to dawn on her that she was living a story she did not want to tell. By that time, however, she did not know how to extricate herself or how to make Jen a lesser character in the cast of her life.

Learn to Question What You Are Thinking

This is not an uncommon situation. Women are such emotional beings, and our longings for connection are great; therefore, it is easy to be drawn away to whatever pool of feeling seems deep. As you are reading this, you may even be recognizing your own story. So often we wake up where we never intended to go because we proceeded headlong without asking, "What am I thinking?" Failing to question if this is the way you want your story to read leads to a lot of unnecessary heartache that could have been different if a few questions had been asked.

Learn the Art of Asking Questions

There came a time in my life when I learned the art of asking myself questions. It was a moment when I needed someone to query what was going on in my head. None of my friends questioned me because they all seemed to see things the same way. Everyone I knew thought as I did, so it never occurred to me to think any differently. The way I was thinking, though, was not taking me anywhere. I was stuck in a relational quagmire that just seemed to sit and fester.

It finally occurred to me that, if you do not question what you think, you automatically assume it is right. Stopping to ask yourself why you are doing what you are doing or thinking what you are thinking sometimes gives you a great breather that allows you the time to stand back and look at things in a different way.

At the time of my *aha!* moment, I was in ministry and had become a student of the Bible. A lot of my beliefs had been solidified, but I was still growing in my understanding of relationships. I had just never thought about what a healthy friendship really looked like. I had never questioned it. In my mind, I was doing what was right, so why should I question it? Then I found myself caught in a scenario from which I thought there was no reasonable exit. What seemed like a good relationship at the start had become painful and difficult. I believed if I did what was right, everything would turn out okay. But I was stuck. I did not know the questions to ask. I did not know the answers to give. I just did not know. I was still writing a story, but it was not saying what I wanted it to say.

Then along came Marie Chapian, therapist and author of

Telling Yourself the Truth. (This was a book I had on my shelf for a long time and never bothered to read, primarily because I thought I *knew* the truth.) Marie and I met in a recording studio. We had a delightful interview, and afterward there was a lot of small talk around the studio table. Someone asked an innocuous question, and I broke out in very uncharacteristic tears. Because of the way I reacted, Marie said, "Oh, my dear, God has sent me here for you." I had no idea what that would mean, but I was so glad God knew where I was, what I needed, and had sent someone to help me.

Looking back, I now know this was when it first became abundantly clear God has a huge part in our stories. We do not often see what a big part He plays and how attuned He really is to our lives, but He *is* there! When I met with Marie, she immediately began to question me and encourage me to ask myself questions. Her goal was getting me unstuck from my belief system that clearly had me bound. It was time for a new story. I no longer needed to live with thinking that was taking me nowhere and causing pain not only to me but also to others.

For the next year, Marie carefully challenged me on everything I thought and nudged me toward learning to question myself. It was through that process I caught on to a way of thinking and doing life that would allow me to write a new story without completely wiping out the old one. I came to the realization that stories in our lives are like seasons—they come and go. Some come in with gale-force winds, and the change between the old and new is dramatic. Some come in on gentler breezes, and the change is not as noticeable until one day it is too warm for the thinking we have clung to for so many months. We just don't need it any more.

Where Is That Written?

I have learned to question what I think, what other people say and question, and what I really believe. If we never ask, we will never get answers. One of my favorite questions is, "Where is that written?" It covers a multitude of questions because so much of what we are told either is not written or is not written the way it is interpreted. Have you ever heard anyone say, "I just haven't prayed enough"? My question is, "How much is enough?" Or have you ever heard anyone say, "This is really going to be a wonderful event because there has been so much opposition"? My question is, "Where is that written?" Just because things are messed up and people have run into some obstacles, does that guarantee that God is going to move in extraordinary ways? Is that truth, or is that assumption? When we *assume*, we often miss the real truth and can put ourselves in bondage, which is never a nice story even when the assumptions are benign.

Knowing truth is such a huge issue and seems to be becoming much more so in our culture. If we do not write our stories based on God's truth, then we set ourselves up for stories we do not want to tell. No matter whether you are young and just starting out or you are more seasoned and have written many chapters, truth matters. You may seek truth in different ways, but the goal is always to ask ourselves the critical question, "Where is that written?"

My friend Sheri Schulze is an amazing woman who embraces truth with a capital T. She has raised three wonderful daughters. In the process, she and another mom used every tool at hand to teach their girls how to recognize truth. One afternoon, several of the girls were gathered in Sheri's kitchen. She told them they were going to bake a cake. She had laid out the ingredients from a *corrupted* recipe she had made up. She changed the amount of salt they would put in the recipe. The girls happily and blindly put all of the ingredients together and then put the cake in the oven.

During the wait for the cake to bake, Sheri led them in a Bible study and a discussion of truth—how to find it, how to recognize it, and the questions they needed to learn to ask. After some lively interaction with the girls, it was time for the cake. Sheri had taken it out of the oven and let it cool while they talked. Now it was time to serve it. Each girl took a large piece and bit into it. The looks on their faces were priceless as they reacted to what they believed was a wonderful, fresh, homemade piece of cake. It looked good, it smelled good, but the taste, which is the measure of a cake, was terrible. Gag! What was wrong?

The recipe was corrupted, and no one had questioned the inordinate amount of salt. No one had said, "Are you sure?" No one had asked, "Is this truly a cake recipe?" "What's up, Mrs. Schulze?" Lesson learned. The discussion became livelier as they talked about how they had been deceived and did not know it. Of course, Sheri had baked another cake earlier with a truthful recipe. The girls ate it with great delight. More than learning to check out the ingredient amounts in recipes, they had learned the great lesson that truth, not assumptions, is what gives you good results.

Rahab the Harlot

If we take a minute and go to the Scriptures, we will meet a dear woman whose life and the lives of her family depended on her recognizing truth and believing it. Her story could have gone either way, and the way she chose determined her life or death.

The woman's name was Rahab. She appeared early in the book of Joshua. I am not sure we would think of her as a woman whose story depended on truth because the other name she went by was "the harlot."

Let me give you a little of her backstory. The children of Israel were on the move. God was leading them into the promised land. This was the second generation to go on this journey. The first generation, led by Moses, escaped Egypt and confidently headed toward the territory they had been given, but they failed to get there, basically because of their attitude. They did not rely on the truth they knew. They let their minds run wild, and the story they could have written ended with shame and defeat. There is an interesting commentary on the first generation in 1 Corinthians 10: "Brothers and sisters, I want you to know what happened to our ancestors who followed Moses . . . God was not pleased with most of them, so they died in the desert" (vv. 1, 5).

The generation led by Moses either died early or was left to wander in the desert until they finally died. God then raised up Joshua to lead the next generation. He was a warrior who told the people, "Be strong and courageous! Do not tremble or be dismayed, for the LORD your God is with you wherever you go" (Josh. 1:9 NASB). It was not going to be easy. They were now being allowed to enter the land, but they would have to conquer cities and eliminate the enemies of Jehovah before they could get there. The Canaanites were a well-entrenched people who would not give up their cities easily. Jericho was the first Canaanite town they had to conquer on their march. Rahab lived in a house built on the wall that surrounded the city.

We meet Rahab in the story when she hid two spies sent by Joshua to investigate her town. When asked if she knew their whereabouts, she lied to the king's envoys. That could be an ethical issue for you if you are not practiced in discerning the overarching truths that make up God's story. Do not let that stop you as you look for the truth that Rahab believed and relied upon to support her actions. See if you can explain why truth triumphs even if the picture is murky.

Before Joshua started his trip into the promised land, he had sent two spies to check out the land, especially the city of Jericho. The two men entered the city before the gates closed and made their way to the most hospitable house in the town—the home of Rahab the harlot. She invited them in and hid them because word on the street was that the king of the city was on the hunt to "spy out the spies."

Houses during that time had flat roofs used for extra sleeping areas, storage, and a cool place to sit during the evening. Rahab sent the young men to the roof and hid them under some stalks of flax stored on the roof.

The king's men did, indeed, come looking for the two spies, but Rahab was discerning enough to know she would be badly mistaken to turn them in. After she sent the king's men on a wild goose chase, she went up to the roof where she had hidden the spies.

Before the spies went to sleep for the night, Rahab went up to the roof. She said to them, "I know the LORD has given this land to your people. You frighten us very much. Everyone living in this land is terribly afraid of you because we have heard how the LORD dried up the Red Sea when you came out of Egypt. We have heard how you destroyed Sihon and Og, two Amorite kings who lived east of the Jordan. When we heard this, we were very frightened. Now our men are afraid to fight you because the

LORD your God rules the heavens above and the earth below! So now, promise me before the LORD that you will show kindness to my family just as I showed kindness to you. Give me some proof that you will do this. Allow my father, mother, brothers, sisters, and all of their families to live. Save us from death." (2:8–13)

Wow! Did she say a mouthful? She stated her whole belief about God and what He could do. As far as she was concerned, He ruled "the heavens above and the earth below." She was willing to bet her life and the lives of her family on it. It was that basic. She believed it, and she was not too proud to ask the two young men to "save us from death."

The men agreed and said, "It will be our lives for your lives if you don't tell anyone what we are doing. When the LORD gives us the land, we will be kind and true to you."

The house Rahab lived in was built on the city wall, so she used a rope to let the men down through a window. She said to them, "Go into the hills so the king's men will not find you. Hide there for three days. After the king's men return, you may go on your way."

The men said to her, "You must do as we say. If not, we cannot be responsible for keeping this oath you have made us swear. When we return to this land, you must tie this red rope in the window through which you let us down. Bring your father, mother, brothers, and all your family into your house. If anyone leaves your house and is killed, it is his own fault. We cannot be responsible for him. If anyone in your house is hurt, we will be responsible. But if you tell anyone about this, we will be free from the oath you made us swear."

Rahab answered, "I agree to this." So she sent them away, and they left. Then she tied the red rope in the window. (vv. 14–21)

The king and his men searched the roads around Jericho for three days. Then they returned to their little fortified city without finding the men. Meanwhile, the spies found their way back to Joshua and gave him the good report about the land. They said, "The LORD surely has given us all of the land. All the people in that land are terribly afraid of us" (v. 24).

There could have been many people who knew the truth and were afraid but were killed anyway. Rahab's believing it enough to bank her life on it saved her. Ask her family what they thought about her outrageous faith in the "God in heaven and earth." When the Israelites were quietly walking around the city for six days, can you imagine what the people inside those walls were thinking? Ponder that one as we proceed.

Several years ago I stayed in a lovely Southern bed-and-breakfast. I was the only guest that night, and there was time to chat with the proprietress, who was about my age. As women do, we shared our stories—what we did, where we had been, what we liked, what we did not like—and as we got to know each other better, we went a little deeper. She had lovely gardens around her beautiful old antebellum home. She had meticulously manicured them, and they spoke of being carefully attended, but as I got to know her in that one-time conversation, I recognized a life and a mind-set that were well manicured as well.

We will call her Bonita, and this is her story: She had been married many years to a man who decided he was in love with someone else. They tried to put the marriage back together after he sent his paramour packing, but things never were the same. He was restless and disinterested, so finally she released him to go. Concurrent with his departure, Bonita became very ill. If that were all I knew of her story, I would have thought, *Despair and loss, how sad.* But there was more. Life as she had known it was crumbling in front of her eyes, but God had some more chapters for her to live and more gardens for her to groom. She miraculously survived her illness, and with the settlement from the divorce, she found a wonderful old house that, like her, seemed to be begging for attention and renovation. Something that drew her to the property was the abundance of old gardens that were languishing from lack of nurturing as well.

She decided this would begin the rest of her story. Today, several years later, her bed-and-breakfast is a going concern, surrounded by showcase gardens that she has loved and manicured with the attention of a master gardener.

As I sat and talked with her, I was amazed at her resilience, lack of bitterness, and focus on the future. The many years with her husband had surely been significant, but the new life she was living was a picture of choosing to dig, root out, and replant. Bonita got a life when it looked as if the one she was living had been taken away from her. If she had to say, I sensed that she would have told you the life she lives now is a far better life than the one she lived for those many years that seemed so normal to her neighbors and the townsfolk. They find her pretty interesting now. They know her survivor story, but they are more enamored with her house, her gardens, and the woman she has become. No one ever dreamed she had it in her!

I sensed that she was a woman who had asked herself some hard questions and had found some answers at great cost. It would have been so much easier for her to have lived an "unquestioned" life. It would have saved her the nerve it took to start again when it looked as if life was over. She questioned and found that answers she had never thought of were just waiting to be discovered.

Troubled or Tranquil?

Jesus' friend Martha has a short little episode recorded in the Scriptures. (Aren't you glad your life drama will not be told in the Bible for everybody in the world, both now and in the future, to read?)

> While Jesus and his followers were traveling, Jesus went into a town. A woman named Martha let Jesus stay at her house. Martha had a sister named Mary, who was sitting at Jesus' feet and listening to him teach. But Martha was busy with all the work to be done. She went in and said, "Lord, don't you care that my sister has left me alone to do all the work? Tell her to help me."
>
> But the Lord answered her, "Martha, Martha, you are worried and upset about many things. Only one thing is important. Mary has chosen the better thing, and it will never be taken away from her." (Luke 10:38–42)

Martha was a woman in charge, yet because of her troubled thinking, Jesus had to point out to her that she was bothered about many things, and as a result, she was missing out on the better part of life. Her sister, Mary, had a beautiful story of peace and quietness that Martha could not write. She was missing it. I have missed it too. I understand. Maybe you have, as well, but it is a story that can be written when we actually look at what is filling our minds and we ask ourselves the questions we need to ask:

- Why does this bother you so much?
- Why does what so-and-so thinks matter to you so much?
- Why are you worried about this?
- What good will it do for you to worry?
- What are you thinking anyway?
- How is this helping your story?
- Is this the story you want everyone to read about you?
- Are you believing the truth or are you making assumptions?

My friend Lynda Elliott has a unique perspective on life. As a former social worker, she worked for years in the field of child abuse and saw many people whose lives reeked of death—death to their dreams, death to their hopes, and often death to their relationships. If any group of people needed to find the truth and a way to write new stories in their lives, it was this group. Instead of throwing up her hands at the seeming hopelessness of it all, Lynda always seemed to see the bright side and a way to look at things differently. Lynda's experience aptly describes the kernel of hope—and, therefore, life—that can be found even in what seems like a hopeless situation.

These are Lynda's words:

Sometimes, we don't even know we have a choice to make. When I worked in child abuse, I met my first client, Sally, who had been battered by her husband. She had bruises on her neck and cuts inside her right cheek because her husband had choked her and then backhanded her. As we began to talk, she told me she was abused by her father when she was a child, but she had married her present husband, Scott, when she was fifteen so she could escape her father's abuse. When they married, he had never hit anybody. She could not understand how she married someone who later would also abuse her.

When I met her husband, Scott, who was a small guy, I could hardly imagine him hitting her. Scott was mild-mannered and shy. When I asked him to tell me what preceded his hitting her, this is what he said: "I told her that I needed some peace and quiet after work. I work hard, long hours, and I just need time to drink a beer, read the newspaper, and cool down. I told her that if I could just relax for a little while, we could have a nice family evening. She would go along with me for weeks at a time, keeping the kids quiet while she cooked supper. Everything would be fine, but then she would get steamed up over something and just start up again. She would circle my chair as I read the paper, complaining about our financial situation or the behavior of the kids."

He continued, "I would warn her, but she just kept on until finally she would pull the paper down and get in my face. I warned her again, but she kept on until I finally hit her a few times."

When I met with them together, I asked him to tell his story again and asked her if it was true. She admitted that it was totally true. I asked her how she felt the moment after he hit her. She replied, "Satisfied."

From meeting that couple, I learned that we can become attached to our pain. No matter how much we hate it, we can miss it when it's gone. We don't feel quite right until we find a way to hurt again.

Seeing the truth gives us new opportunity. As Scott and Sally began to see their pain cycle, they had to decide whether or not they would choose pain or peace. Scott realized that no matter how Sally might behave she did not deserve to be beaten. When Sally caught a glimpse of another way to live, she had to decide to give up her pain-seeking behavior and learn how to choose love rather than pain. It took time and courage, but each step made her stronger. As Sally began to experience peace instead of the pain of abuse, she became more and more confident that love was definitely the choice to make.

The Freedom of Truth

Knowing and believing the truth is the catalyst for writing a new story. Truth propels us toward freedom. "Then you will know the truth, and the truth will make you free" (John 8:32). Jesus spoke these words when he was addressing the Jews who had believed Him. They questioned why they needed to be free. They claimed they had never been in bondage to anyone because they were descendents of Abraham. Jesus immediately cut to the truth of the situation. It had nothing to do with their heritage from Abraham but their slavery to sin. He was opening their eyes to a new way of living. The old understanding had to be replaced. He was giving them truth that could give them a new story. "So if the Son makes you free, you will be truly free" (John 8:36).

Knowing and believing the truth is the catalyst for writing a new story.

70

Truth is the bedrock of a new story. Once we see the faulty, non-functioning nature of our old tales or even the error in old chapters, we can move forward, start to change, and find freedom. You could even find life, a life you have never known before. That is what happened to our friend Rahab. She was a harlot who kept a guest house in the city of Jericho. She was surrounded by people who worshipped Canaanite gods and who, by the way, made human sacrifices to the god Molech. They were not the nicest bunch in the world, but they were redeemable, if they had wanted to be redeemed. But watch and see how they behaved. Here's what happened next:

> The people of Jericho were afraid because the Israelites were near. They closed the city gates and guarded them. No one went into the city, and no one came out.
>
> Then the LORD said to Joshua, "Look, I have given you Jericho, its king, and all its fighting men. March around the city with your army once a day for six days. Have seven priests carry trumpets made from horns of male sheep and have them march in front of the Ark. On the seventh day march around the city seven times and have the priests blow the trumpets as they march. They will make one long blast on the trumpets. When you hear that sound, have all the people give a loud shout. Then the walls of the city will fall so the people can go straight into the city." (Josh. 6:1–5)

And that is exactly what they did. One day, two days, three days, quietly marching around the city once each day. Four days, five days, six days, and then on the seventh day, the silent Israelites marched around the city seven times and suddenly erupted into shouts as the priests blew on their trumpets. Amazingly, the walls fell flat, so they could walk right over them and into the city.

While all that tumult and mayhem was going on, there was a woman named Rahab and her family clinging to a red rope (remember her deal with the spies?), believing they would be rescued and set free.

As it is in so many stories, there is the scene we see, and there's the scene God is writing that we cannot see. Rahab's story is one of those. She believed the truth about God, and that changed her life story and the story of her family. Little did she know what God's plans were. The harlot who lived in a house on the wall in Jericho was to become a major player in a much greater story. God had His plan in place, and as Job acknowledged when he answered God, "I know that you can do all things and that no plan of yours can be ruined" (Job 42:2).

The Other Mother-in-Law

Remember our girl Ruth from Chapter 1, who loved her mother-in-law, Naomi, and followed her to Bethlehem? Well, Rahab from Jericho played a part in Ruth's story that few people mention. Rahab was Ruth's *other* mother-in-law. It's true. Who would have thought it? Perhaps death prevented them from ever meeting in this life; we cannot know for sure. What we do know from the Scriptures, though, is that Rahab left a godly legacy. That is quite a statement about an ex-harlot from a godless, decadent city in the middle of the desert!

You have seen the main chronicle of Rahab's life in the book of Joshua, but her legacy of faith draws comments elsewhere in God's Word, which we can see by piecing together the family connection.

This is fun. Now that you know both Ruth and Rahab, it is like putting together a genealogical puzzle. (Have you ever done that for yourself? You might find some interesting pieces to your story too.) Let's begin back in Ruth's story:

> The women told Naomi, "Praise the LORD who gave you this grandson. May he become famous in Israel. He will give you new life and will take care of you in your old age because of your daughter-in-law [Ruth] who loves you. She is better for you than seven sons, because she has given birth to your grandson."
>
> *Rahab left a godly legacy. That is quite a statement about an ex-harlot from a godless, decadent city in the middle of the desert!*
>
> Naomi took the boy, held him in her arms, and cared for him. The neighbors gave the boy his name, saying, "This boy was born for Naomi." They named him Obed. Obed was the father of Jesse, and Jesse was the father of David.
>
> This is the family history of Perez, the father of Hezron. Hezron was the father of Ram, who was the father of Amminadab. Amminadab was the father of Nahshon, who was the father of Salmon. Salmon was the father of Boaz, who was the father of Obed. Obed was the father of Jesse, and Jesse was the father of David. (Ruth 4:14–22)

Based on those verses, and to see the genealogy clearly, answer these questions before we go on:

- Who did Ruth marry?
- What does this text tell us about her family and extended family?
- Naomi was her mother-in-law. Who was her father-in-law?
- Who was her son?
- Who was her grandson?
- Who was her great-grandson?

Now, look at part of the genealogy of Jesus Christ that Matthew 1:1–6 records:

> This is the family history of Jesus Christ. He came from the family of David, and David came from the family of Abraham . . .
>> Salmon was the father of Boaz.
>>> (Boaz's mother was Rahab.)
>> Boaz was the father of Obed.
>>> (Obed's mother was Ruth.)
>> Obed was the father of Jesse.
>> Jesse was the father of King David.
>> David was the father of Solomon.

Ruth married Boaz. And who does this scripture say was Boaz's mother? Right, Rahab (v. 5). So Ruth's first mother-in-law was Naomi, and her second mother-in-law was Rahab. And they were both in the lineage of the Savior of the world. Not a bad new story for a former harlot!

Rahab and the people of Jericho started with the same information about God, but while the rest melted in fear, Rahab wrote a new story, aligning with the One she recognized to be "God in heaven above and on earth beneath," and it made all the difference.

Personal Reflection

1. If you could write your own legacy for generations yet unborn, what would it be?
2. Write your own summary statement about what you believe about God.
3. Try to make a list of ten life truths you know for sure.
4. How have these truths affected the way you have lived your life so far?
5. What part have they played in your story?
6. Is there any particular truth that brought you to the need for a new story?
7. Are there any truths about God you are resisting? If so, what are they?
8. What truths about God do you need to acknowledge and submit to in writing your story?
9. Who else might be affected for good as you begin writing your new story?

Journal Entry

To continue your new story, complete the following starter sentence in your personal journal. Then continue writing thoughts and feelings from your heart as long as you need to.

Based on the story of Rahab, I believe I can begin my new story because . . .

Group Discussion Questions

1. How does Rahab's knowledge of God differ from the others in Jericho?

2. Does Rahab know anything the others do not know? What makes you say yes or no?

3. What are some truths you think Rahab came to understand from her encounter with God's spies?

4. If God could use Rahab, a known harlot, in the lineage of His only Son, what does that mean about you?

5. Have you ever heard someone say, "I've done too many bad things for God to forgive me"? If so, how could you use Rahab's story to help them?

6. What other lessons did you learn from the story of Rahab?

7. What are some of the good questions you can ask yourself to begin your new story?

8. What happened when Rahab changed her way of thinking?

Chapter 4

CHANGE YOUR "I CAN'T" TO "I CAN"

Stories can conquer fear, you know. They can make the heart bigger.

—Ben Okri

Deborah

Deborah answered "I can" when God
called her to lead in a culture not
affirming to women.

JUDGES 4–5

The prophetess Deborah was well known among her people as a wise and discerning woman. A woman of courage. A woman of faith. A leader. In fact, she sat under a tree named for her, Palm Tree of Deborah, on a mountainside, and people came from far and near so she could help them solve their problems.

Still, in those days, and in Deborah's culture, women were not highly esteemed . . . except by God. And in the midst of troubling times, God called Deborah to write a new story for her life. He took her away from her comfortable shade tree and ordered her into a man's battle.

Deborah was known for her wisdom, so when she told Barak, the commander of the army, that God wanted him to go into battle, it really was not surprising that he did not want to go without her. It also was not surprising that she agreed to go but assured him that he would not receive the glory for their victory.

Her words still ring through my head. My mother repeated them to me many times in my growing up years: "'I can't never could do anything." She usually said them when I began to whine about something that seemed too hard, or when I did not want to do it. It stuck with me, and once I became an adult, if I wanted to do something, I was convinced I could. Unfortunately, that "I can" did not include trigonometry. I never wanted to do that, but I knew I had to pass three quarters to graduate college. (It only took me five quarters to pass that three-quarter course!) I saw no reason for mastering this difficult, irrelevant subject, and to be honest, when I sat down to work my way through the textbook, there was a big "I can't" in front of my eyes. Usually there is a story behind an "I can't," and there is one behind mine.

When I was in the third grade, my fine motor skills were not very well developed. I did not do well writing neat papers, especially math papers. I did not have straight lines or regularly shaped numbers. I did the best I could, but my best did not measure up to my teacher's rigorous demands. One day before we left for home, Miss Mason held my paper up in front of the class and said, "This is the kind of paper I never want to see!" My name was scrawled across the top. There was no doubt it was mine. I was horrified and, I think, a little scared. What was she going to do to me?

Having made her statement, she laid the paper on my desk and dismissed the class for the day. Everyone went home, including me, but I took with me a strong message—"You can't do arithmetic." From that day forward I harbored the belief that I could not do math. It followed me through high school and college. If I were going to have a rough time, you could count on it being in math. Even after I graduated from college, I had dreams about failing that last test in trigonometry. I dreamed I went forward to get my diploma and was denied because I did not pass math. So "I can't" really could not do anything. I was convinced it was beyond me. Although I could do a lot of things, I could not pass math.

Now that I am older and have had some experience, I have discovered I *can* do math. I delight in trying to figure out mathematical problems, although I admit Sudoku gives me heartburn. I think I could even do that, if I wanted to. I just do not want to!

Birth of a New Attitude

"I can" is an important phrase to embrace because life is full of challenges that seem much too hard. I was talking with a young first-time mother recently. She said, "You know, you get in that birthing room, and it occurs to you that no one is going to come take over your labor when you get too tired. It is yours to do, and you have to do it!" I would say that is an epiphany of "I can"!

Rodney, my hairstylist and one of my favorite people, lost his dad recently. His death was sudden and unexpected. As I visited with him and his sister Pam at the funeral home, Rodney said, "I didn't think I could do this, but the grace of God has been around us. We have been able to do what we had to do."

Pam agreed. "You never could have told me that we could go through this without caving in, but God's grace has been all around us." They both had seen the reality of "Do what you have to do, and God gets you through." They both learned they could do what they never thought they could do.

The women who make it are those who have decided, "In spite of it all, I can and I will."

It is easier to say, "I can't" than it is to say, "I can." "I can't" requires no effort. "I can" requires knowledge of what you can do and how well you can do it. It also reveals how determined you are to do what you *can do*, rather than languishing in the swamp of what you *can't do*.

A new narrative often emerges from "I can" because it must. I have noticed that many new stories are not voluntary; they are created out of circumstances that require a strong "I can" to survive. The women who make it are those who have decided, "In spite of it all, I can and I will."

One of my friends is just such a girl. Abandoned by her husband and left with children to rear, she determined to say, "I will." She managed to go back to school, get her undergraduate and master's degrees, and she now is helping her children get through college. She has *decluttered* her life, leaving the old house, the old stuff, and the old story behind, and she is looking to the future while encouraging her four children to do the same.

If she had said, "I can't," her family would still be sitting in the old house with the old stuff, lamenting what might have been if their father had not bailed on them. As it is, they do not like what he did, but they are not victims of it either. Their mother not only told them, but she also showed them that you are only a victim when you *think* you are a victim. Bad things happen, but you do not have to let them define your life. You do not have to let them embed "I can't" into your head for the rest of your days. You can write your own story; you do not have to let someone else do it. God's story is bigger than yours, and He loves it when you get in stride with Him and do not let the bad times take you down. He is all about *getting through* and *taking you up higher* and *running the race to win*.

Learned Helplessness

"Learned helplessness" is a phrase that caught my attention a couple of years ago when I began to read about the new field of positive psychology. I say "new" because, unlike the old Freudian model, it focuses on what makes people mentally *healthy* and not mentally *ill*. Dr. Martin Seligman, who has been deemed the father of positive psychology, believes, "Having options and making choices is the very foundation of human psychological health."[1]

You are only a victim when you think you are a victim.

"Life can be brutal," he says, "but if we always have options, we'll always have hope."[2] Learned helplessness, or the pain of "I can't," can overtake almost anyone. "It most often occurs in three basic situations: when someone fails too many times, when someone is boxed in by a double-bind, lose-lose situation, or when someone is dominated by somebody else who takes away his opportunity to choose."[3]

Focusing on strengths rather than weaknesses gives each of us a chance to move forward with personal self-talk that is invigorating. Anytime we say to ourselves, "I can't," a weakening sets into our constitution. In fact, when we feel helpless and tell ourselves "I can't," whole bodies often see chemistry changes. The contentment neurotransmitters serotonin and dopamine are depleted, and we are left with a perpetual state of "I can't."[4]

Exercise has never appealed to me. I have never understood people who love it and cannot live without it. I do not mind walking, lifting a few weights, and staying busy around the house, but the thought of joining a class and exercising has given me the hives all my life. Richard Simmons annoys me with his enthusiasm, and honestly the thought of "sweating to the oldies" is gross. I had a big "I can't" in my head when it came to group exercise. Like most things, I can track that "I can't" back to childhood. Believe it or not, it happened with my mother, the queen of "I can."

Mother was also my fifth grade teacher, and I remember as if it were yesterday the moment I thought, *I can't*. We were having tumbling as our physical education activity. Keep in mind that when I was in the fifth grade, I was almost as tall as I am today—five foot eight. Most of the other girls were still tiny and nimble, but I had the body of an almost full-grown woman. I am sure Mother was thinking about the awkwardness my rolling around the floor would present for us all, so she gave me the drum to beat during the tumbling class. (I think it was for keeping time, but who really knows?) No one ever said anything. I beat the drum, and the other kids tumbled, but the message I got was, "I can't," and so I never did! The very thought of group exercise was relegated to the "I can't" bucket, and the years rolled on without that being an issue.

In this time of life, however, and in this culture, group exercise is something we cannot avoid considering! I want to be healthy, and the chance to be part of a group of women my age who are exercising at the local sports club became too enticing. So with fear and trepidation I signed up, stepping over the "I can't" that always seemed to be there, and have found a whole new world of fun, fitness, and fellowship! (I even have to alliterate to describe it—an almost poetic experience.) I never thought the words *I like this* would come out of my mouth in the same sentence as *exercise*, but now they have. I am writing a new story about exercise and other physical issues. High fructose corn syrup is history in my new story, as well as white bread and trans fats. I drink water and green tea, and the thought of a diet soft drink gags me. This has been a slowly emerging new story, but it has been a good one, creating a healthier future.

The "I Can" Purpose

All of us have "I can'ts" to overcome. I believe it is one reason why God gave us His Spirit, to remind us of "I can" when the old self-talk bogs us down with the "I can'ts." If you start living your life empowered by the Spirit of God, you may recognize for the first time that your story is really about the continuing presence of Christ and His involvement in everything you do.

If God has gifted you and given you an outlet for that gift, your job is to go through the doors He opens, believing that He really does have a plan He wants to accomplish through you. Even if you are in a job that seems to have no purpose, or you have to leave a place where you had some prestige, He has a purpose. If today you are feeling frumpy and useless, or if there is an exercise class you have been avoiding although you know it has your name on it, God has a plan.

Writing a new story puts a new perspective on every event in your life. If you know that God is in the middle of all that you do, every relationship you have, and every challenge that faces you, then somehow you can believe that there is purpose and you have been given everything you need to fulfill that purpose. The *how* and the *why* may be a mystery to you, but God knows, God cares, and He is at work. When you say, "I can," you are just affirming what the Spirit of God is telling you.

I hear your question: what if you are *not* supposed to do something you have set out to do? You are aware that a mindless "I can" will lead you down a wrong road every time. No doubt about it. But if you will relax into the fact that God has the big story under His control, and that He is perfectly capable of putting up roadblocks if you go too far down a wrong path, then you can relax and live! I am convinced that too often we get tangled up trying to outthink God. You can think something negative or someone, anyone, can say something less than encouraging, and that negative becomes the overarching principle of your life. That kind of reasoning will lead to a bad case of the "I can'ts."

I had lunch recently with a young woman I believe in so much. She is bright, gifted, deep of spirit, and generous of heart. She ministers from a well of past experience and healed pain. Her effectiveness is without question, but for years she has held herself back. Someone close to her told her that God would not be pleased if she outgrew the spiritual depth of her husband. She believed it and set out to make *him* grow.

He is a kind, hardworking, precious man, but he is not the powerhouse his wife is. He loves her, supports what she does, and believes in her, but he does not want to do what she does. Thinking she had to make him catch up to her passion, she used everything she had in her persuasive powers to make it happen, but he is who he is, and he is content. She is who she is, and she finally has abandoned her job of pushing and pulling. She saw the fallacy of the advice given to her with all goodwill but had disastrous results. She now has let her husband be himself (what a relief for him), and she has become herself—flying and soaring in God's great plan for her. "I can" permeates her being now. She is not holding herself back with any false religious restraints. She recognizes her strengths and gifts and glories in them for the glory of God.

Two New Stories Intersect

A new story emerges with power and great impact when we focus on our strengths and recognize that we are made for the moment in which we live and are gifted to make a difference in our own corner of the world. As the wonderful old hymn title suggests, "Brighten the Corner Where You Are." You do not have to figure it out; you can just know that often God uses the *unlikely* to accomplish the *impossible*.

Kay Arthur, the originator of Precept Inductive Bible Studies, has always been a picture of the unlikely with whom God has done the impossible. Kay's story is one that no one could have dreamed up. In her late twenties, she was living the life of a man-starved divorcée when God apprehended her and dramatically changed her story. At a desperate love-deficit moment in her own life, she cried out to God, and He met her. He changed her life, changed her world, and changed her direction. He called her out of the darkness of her old story, which involved the suicide of her first husband, her dalliance with a married man, and her desperate search for unconditional acceptance.

He saved her from herself and forgave her sins. He put a passion to know Him in her heart and then amazingly took a woman whose formal education was limited to a nursing degree and turned her into one of the world's leading biblical scholars and proponents of inductive Bible study. The scope of her influence reaches around the world today as she continues to write her new story. To say that she is the *improbable* doing the *impossible* may be an understatement. That is the delight of living in a new story. Kay would be the first to say that she did not plan to live her adult life the way she has lived it, but it was clear that God had other plans. He gave her the *how to* and *want to* for doing His good pleasure, and she has stayed at it with passion all these years.

God uses the unlikely to accomplish the impossible.

Kay's life intersected with mine, and God wrote a script I had no idea I would read. Kay and I met "by chance" in the seventies, and it seemed that from the beginning God had a plan for our lives. I came alongside and did whatever needed to be done in the early days of Kay's Bible study ministry. I tackled the nursery, the tape ministry, the newsletter, the receptionist position, and from time to time acted as an assistant to Kay. I learned volumes while I was doing all of this, but I had no idea what it would mean for my future.

Kay began to use me as a substitute teacher. I had won some speaking contests in high school, so I was not unfamiliar with public speaking, but I was totally unaware that I was about to be thrown into an arena to speak before thousands of women. I did not know that this was a strength I had, but I believed "I can," and I did it. My real baptism into the speaking world was a Wednesday in September when Kay was leading a tour in the Holy Land for two weeks. She asked me to introduce the book of John to her Bible study class of sixteen hundred women in Atlanta. With fear and many lost nights of sleep, I did it. I believed I could, but I had never taught that many women before. Two hundred had been my max.

On that day as I looked out on that sea of unfamiliar faces, my knees went weak. Then the emcee announced that Kay Arthur would not be there to teach that day. Sixteen hundred women corporately sighed their disappointment with a pro- longed "Ohhhhhh." Then the emcee said, "But Jan Silvious is," which was followed by a profound, prolonged silence. That was the true beginning of my new story of speaking and writing. I began as Kay Arthur's substitute.

A couple of years later the request calls began to come in for me. My calling was not always to be Kay's substitute, although I was honored to fill in for her, but it was to be the life God planned for *me*. I had come from being a fearful, depressed wife and mother in one world into a world I had never known or dreamed of. I had a new life, and the choice was before me: live it with the fears and unknowns, as well as the joys and adventures, or stay where I was. The Spirit of God is not demanding. He is at all times a gentleman and will never cross your free will. You can choose the safe, the secure, and the known, or you can choose the big mysteries and the quests and treasures of walking a new story with Him.

Deborah—the "I Can" Judge

One of my favorite scriptures records the "I can" of Deborah, a woman who easily could have said, "I can't." She lived in a rough, unpredictable time.

The people of Israel had become a very disorganized, loose confederacy after their conquest of Canaan under Joshua. Therefore, without leadership, they repeatedly fell into idolatry, foreign political domination, intermarriage with pagans, and other major sins. They were in a general state of spiritual confusion. They needed help. So God raised up "judges," although the better translation of the Hebrew word is "heroes" (and "heroines").[5]

So Deborah was raised up to help, to be a heroine and lead the people. She was a woman with a husband and a household, living in a culture that did not really value women. God, however, had gifted her and called her. She had to lead. And lead she did! She fulfilled the plan God had for her even though it did not line up with what all the other women of the day were doing. She knew she was called, and it was up to her to answer. Let's get a preview of her powerful story before we move on. This was a woman who said, "I can, and I will!"

> After Ehud died, the Israelites again did what the LORD said was wrong. So he let Jabin, a king of Canaan who ruled in the city of Hazor, defeat Israel. Sisera, who lived in Harosheth Haggoyim, was the commander of Jabin's army. Because he had nine hundred iron chariots and was very cruel to the people of Israel for twenty years, they cried to the LORD for help.

A prophetess named Deborah, the wife of Lappidoth, was judge of Israel at that time. Deborah would sit under the Palm Tree of Deborah, which was between the cities of Ramah and Bethel, in the mountains of Ephraim. And the people of Israel would come to her to settle their arguments. (Judg. 4:1–5)

These were rugged days. The iron chariots were formidable, and the men who used them were cruel. The people needed help and someone to rescue them from the grip of oppression. That may have been one reason they were so grateful for Deborah. When the children of Israel came to Deborah, they obviously recognized that she was a woman of wisdom. They would not have gone up into the mountains of Ephraim to hear the babblings of a self-possessed, foolish woman. She had something they desperately needed, and she freely gave it. They just had to have the humility and grace to take it.

The Trail of Tears

Nancy Ward (*Nanye-hi* in her native tongue) was a woman who had the spirit of "I can" and proved to be an amazing asset to her people, the Cherokee. She could have been our Israelite friend Deborah's first cousin! (Since I am a Tennessean and live in the foothills of the Smoky Mountains, I have a heart for the Cherokee, who were constantly assaulted by other Native American tribes as well as the white man who encroached on their territory.)

This brave woman's husband was killed in a battle while she fought by his side. When she saw that he had been shot, she jumped up from behind a log and yelled for the Cherokee warriors to fight harder. She grabbed a rifle and led her tribal kinsmen in a charge on the Creek warriors, who were fierce fighters. That assault shook the Creek to the core and allowed the Cherokee to win.[6] She was not born a battle commander, but when she faced the job, she said, "I can!" And she did.

On more than one occasion, *Nanye-hi* proved herself to be so brave that the Cherokee nation chose her as *Ghighau* or "Beloved Woman." This was a powerful position that carried a lot of weight in the tribal government "because the Cherokee believed that the Great Spirit frequently spoke through the Beloved Woman."[7]

John Sevier, a hero of the day, found himself being warned and saved on several occasions by *Nanye-hi*, who had taken the name Nancy Ward when she married a white trader. Her help did not seem to matter to him when it came time to discuss the settlement of some of the Cherokee land. He strongly objected to his old ally, *Nanye-hi*, being at the discussions. He thought it was not a place for women. Despite his dismissive attitude toward her, she answered him wisely and eloquently: "You know that women are always looked upon as nothing; but we are your mothers; you are our sons. Our cry is all for peace; let it continue. This peace must last forever. Let your women's sons be ours; our sons be yours. Let your women hear our words."[8]

No matter what your culture, wisdom is something to be coveted, especially, I believe, in women. I have seen that it serves women well to act wisely, especially when they are dealing with men who may have a prejudicial bias against what a woman can do. There are more battles to be won by speaking words of wisdom and behaving wisely than by jumping headlong into a situation with "I can" as your only weapon.

If you recognize your strengths and have the wisdom God

supplies to use them, you will find that you will be able to operate in unusual situations with unique freedom and respect. You will be able to write a new story with energy and anticipation while establishing your position as Beloved Woman. What a lovely title.

Heroine in the Making

It certainly could have been applied to our sister Deborah. She was using her gifts, dispensing wisdom to the people of Israel who came to the hills of Ephraim to see her, when God intervened and changed her story. She was a woman who had what it took to say "I can" with wisdom. Here is what happened when she moved as she believed God had commanded.

Remember, the Israelites were not obeying the Lord, so the Lord had allowed Jabin, a king of Canaan, and Sisera, the commander of his army, to oppress the Israelites with nine hundred iron chariots for twenty years. They cried to the Lord to help them. Enter prophetess and judge Deborah, heroine in the making.

> Deborah would sit under the Palm Tree of Deborah, which was between the cities of Ramah and Bethel, in the mountains of Ephraim. And the people of Israel would come to her to settle their arguments.
>
> Deborah sent a message to Barak son of Abinoam . . . "The LORD, the God of Israel, commands you: 'Go and gather ten thousand men of Naphtali and Zebulun and lead them to Mount Tabor. I will make Sisera, the commander of Jabin's army, and his chariots, and his army, meet you at the Kishon River. I will hand Sisera over to you.'"

Then Barak said to Deborah, "I will go if you will go with me, but if you won't go with me, I won't go." (Judg. 4:5–8)

I have often wondered what was going on in Barak's head. God had commanded him. Deborah had not said she thought the battle was a good idea. She just delivered the message: "'Of course I will go with you,' Deborah answered, 'but you will not get credit for the victory. The LORD will let a woman defeat Sisera'" (v. 9).

Would Deborah be that woman? Good question. Stay tuned because there is more than one woman in this story. It is a mystery indeed.

"So Deborah went with Barak to Kedesh. At Kedesh, Barak called the people of Zebulun and Naphtali together. From them, he gathered ten thousand men to follow him, and Deborah went with him also" (vv. 9–10).

I love this picture. Barak had ten thousand men and Deborah. I bet he would have traded all the men just to keep Deborah by his side.

Then Deborah said to Barak, "Get up! Today is the day the LORD will hand over Sisera. The LORD has already cleared the way for you." So Barak led ten thousand men down Mount Tabor. As Barak approached, the LORD confused Sisera and his army and chariots. The LORD defeated them with the sword, but Sisera left his chariot and ran away on foot. Barak and his men chased Sisera's chariots and army to Harosheth Haggoyim. With their swords they killed all of Sisera's men; not one of them was left alive. (vv. 14–16)

Except, I might add, Sisera. He got out of his chariot and ran away from Barak, who would not go to war without Deborah. Isn't that an interesting combination of valiant men? But wait, it gets more interesting. The scene changes. We go to a remote area where Heber, the Kennite, had pitched a tent in a faraway area of the desert where he lived with his wife, Jael.

Deborah was not the only woman in an atypical situation, facing a very unorthodox chore. If nothing else you have to give Jael (the second woman in this story) credit for creativity when she was faced with her mission. God used two women with "I can" spirits and wisdom to bring about victory. When God declares victory, He means it!

"But Sisera himself ran away to the tent where Jael lived. She was the wife of Heber, one of the Kennite family groups. Heber's family was at peace with Jabin king of Hazor" (v. 17). Sisera thought he was safe because he was in friendly territory—*not!*

Jael went out to meet Sisera and said to him, "Come into my tent, master! Come in. Don't be afraid." So Sisera went into Jael's tent, and she covered him with a rug.

Sisera said to Jael, "I am thirsty. Please give me some water to drink." So she opened a leather bag of milk and gave him a drink. Then she covered him up.

He said to her, "Go stand at the entrance to the tent. If anyone comes and asks you, 'Is anyone here?' say, 'No.'"

But Jael, the wife of Heber, took a tent peg and a hammer and quietly went to Sisera. Since he was very tired, he was in a deep sleep. She hammered the tent peg through the side of Sisera's head and into the ground. And so Sisera died.

At that very moment Barak came by Jael's tent, chasing Sisera. Jael went out to meet him and said, "Come. I will show you the man you are looking for." So Barak entered her tent, and there Sisera lay dead, with the tent peg in his head.

On that day God defeated Jabin king of Canaan in the sight of Israel.

Israel became stronger and stronger against Jabin king of Canaan until finally they destroyed him. (vv. 18–24)

Double Courage Brought Peace

Sometimes it takes two "I cans" in tandem to accomplish God's purposes in our lives. Just as Kay Arthur and I worked together while unknowingly creating new stories, so did Deborah and Jael. You, too, may be teamed up with another "I can" servant of God to achieve the goals the Lord has planned for you. And notice what happened in the long run as a result of these two strong women of God doing what they were assigned to do: "There was peace in the land for forty years" (5:31)!

It is often necessary to go to war in order to create a lasting peace, both on a worldwide scale and in our personal lives. But if we follow God, who is always in control, then He will bring just the right people into our lives at just the right moments to help us win the battles at hand and achieve His plan. As Deborah's song proclaims, "Praise the Lord!"

Personal Reflection

1. Have you ever had an "I can" you felt just *had* to happen?

2. How about your "I can'ts"? What do you think is usually behind them?

3. What does it usually take for you to turn an "I can't" in your life into an "I can"?

4. Where in your life do you see yourself retreating to "I can't"?

5. Who else may be impacted if you change from an "I can't" woman to an "I can" woman? Explain.

6. Do you feel more like a Deborah or a Jael? Why?

7. Do you see yourself leading or "staying in your tent" more willingly? Explain.

8. How will you be able to use Deborah's and Jael's "I cans" to help write your new story this week?

9. Do you wish you could just live in your old story and forget about writing a new one? If so, why?

10. Do you see any hope that changing from "I can't" to "I can" will make a difference in your story?

Journal Entry

To continue your new story, complete the following starter sentence in your personal journal. Then continue writing thoughts and feelings from your heart as long as you need to.

The biggest "I can't" in my life that I want to change to an "I can" is . . .

Group Discussion Questions

1. What historical backdrop hangs behind Deborah's story?
2. Reasoning through the entire text of Judges 4–5, what oppression was Sisera responsible for as commander of Jabin's army? (Take into consideration the phrase in Judges 5:30 that the NCV renders "Each soldier is given a girl or two" in the Hebrew is literally "a womb, a pair of wombs."[9])
3. How did Deborah's "I can" impact Barak? How did it affect the nation of Israel?
4. What do you think was behind Deborah's "I can"?
5. What do you think was behind Barak's "I can't"?
6. Is there a difference between "I can't" and "I don't want to"? If so, what makes the difference?
7. While both Deborah and Jael had ample reason to say, "I can't," each chose to step up when the circumstances of life called for action. Whether you are on the battlefield or in the tent, do you have the ability to choose to respond, "I can"?
8. Why do you feel that Deborah called herself a "mother in Israel"?
9. Although the scene in Jael's tent is gruesome, if you really picture it, what kind of "can do" did she have to display to follow through with dispatching Sisera?
10. What hope do you hear in this story? And what does it mean to us today?

Chapter 5

DELETE THE DRAMA OF THE DAY

If you don't know the trees you may be lost in the forest,
but if you don't know the stories you may be lost in life.

—Anonymous Siberian elder

Hannah

Hannah faced infertility and depression
but resisted the role of Drama Queen.

1 SAMUEL 1:1—2:10

Elkanah had two wives. Now right there you know there's going to be trouble, right? He was married to both Hannah, who had no children, and Peninnah, who had several children. And if that was not enough, Peninnah teased and tormented Hannah mercilessly about her infertility, making Hannah miserable and completely depressed.

Finally, Hannah could stand no more of being beaten up emotionally by "the other woman." So she went to the only place she could think to go—the temple. And there she poured out her broken heart to God, truly the only One who could solve her problem. Eli, the priest, saw her praying passionately and accused her of being drunk. Great! Another emotional blow. Just what she needed. But she convinced him she was just distraught and in urgent prayer. So he blessed her by saying, "May God give you what you have asked."

That's when Hannah's old story turned to a new page, and the results of her sincere prayer impacted a nation for years to come.

Every day brings a new story. For some people, the narrative is living from drama to drama. High tension and big scenes make intense stories that can become addictive. If there is no drama going on, some of us feel as if we are not really living. And while it is true that drama is part of life, God writes a lot of our real story while we focus on chaotic, dramatic scenes being played out under our noses. They demand our attention, but we forget that the bigger narrative being told is greater than our daily soap operas.

Today is when your new story is being written. Worrying about tomorrow or clinging to the what-might-have-been yesterday will stop you dead in your tracks. I have seen whole families consumed with one family member's drama. Day after day the clan is obsessed with what-ifs and oh-nos! about that one person. Because of all the *stuff*, they could easily miss the essence of the day for themselves. Even when legitimate, high-intensity situations exist, the day is still a gift, and God is present. Whether the sun shines brightly or the rain pours in buckets, every twenty-four hours is a special gift to be highly valued.

"But how can I adequately value the days?" you ask.

Keeping good track of your days is a way to value them. We keep careful tabs on our tangible valuables. You know how much *good* jewelry you have and how many pieces of your grandmother's *good* silver are in the silver chest. You have numbered those things because they are precious, maybe even irreplaceable. A good question to ask yourself is, when was the last time I thought about numbering my days? It has probably been a while. It is not something we often do or even hear other people talking about. Numbering your days just means you take a realistic view of the time you have left. You cannot make a totally accurate assessment because you do not know when you will die, but you can estimate your shelf life. Like food, some of us have longer viable days in our lives than others. Some foods last well beyond their expiration dates, and so do some people. Of course, when it comes to

Whether the sun shines brightly or the rain pours in buckets, every twenty-four hours is a special gift to be highly valued.

people, that is God's call, but it is important not to wake up one day wondering why you did not pay attention to your expiration date, wondering why your days that once seemed so long are now so few.

Barring accidents and early onset diseases, the human shelf life, according to the psalmist, is about seventy years, give or take a few years (Ps. 90:10). I think the point is that none of us are going to last forever. Knowing that, each day needs to be embraced and savored as a marvelous gift from God.

Unclutter Your Life

If you want to write a new story with a deeper appreciation for the days you have been given, getting rid of some of the clutter that keeps you from treasuring the hours is important. Drama is one of the biggest time-robbers in life. It can be anything from the stress of a ragged relationship to the nagging whine of people who look to you to fix life for them. Drama can also be a situation you did not cause and cannot possibly fix. It may be obligations you just *assume* are yours to bear. You are not sure what that obligation is totally, but you feel that it is something you are supposed to keep doing. If high drama is your situation, then you could use a new coping strategy called *pushing the Delete button*. This may be the most freeing, gracious thing you can learn to do. I learned this term from a good friend who was responsible for her narcissistic, addicted brother. She spent much money, inordinate amounts of time, and painful concern for several years trying to find the best situation for him. She flew to his aid on many occasions only to rescue him for a few weeks before he returned to his folly. His return to the pit of his self-absorbed, addictive habits was predictable, but she always hoped beyond hope that the *next time* he would escape his personally constructed prison and find life. To this date, he has not done it.

When my friend reached her early sixties, and her brother reached his late fifties, it was as if she had an epiphany. This was taking her life, and each precious day was being consumed with his insanity. She had children, grandchildren, and friends who were being set aside because he was her *drama du jour*. No matter what she did, he managed to show up on the life menu.

It finally occurred to her that she had a Delete button she was not using. She had one on her computer when she needed to clear space to leave room for other things. Why could she not use her personal Delete button and erase his drama from her life? She began to ask herself some good questions: Will I always be compelled to participate in his story? Is it really my obligation? Is this the greater story God has planned for my life? Is this the way I want to spend the precious days I have been given? When she read, "Teach us how short our lives really are so that we may be wise" (Ps. 90:12), she knew what it meant. She finally got it.

If she were going to make the most of the days that she had, she could not spend them continuing to pour her time and treasure into a brother who refused to respond to her help. His ongoing self-absorption was proof enough for her. It was time to push her personal Delete button. Doing so set her free from the ever-present sense of obligation. Her brother's life was his and God's to fix, not hers. Her brother's drama was no longer her focus. It had been for a long time, but she finally saw that her constant attendance at his dramatic show had failed to change one word of his self-destructive script.

If high drama is your situation, then you could use a new coping strategy called pushing the Delete button.

Deleting drama from your life is not easy, but it can be done when you are fighting to protect the precious time we call life. When you have invested time without return and squandered life without any sign of change, you can freely delete the drama. That means you will no longer participate. You turn from watching the dramatist to paying attention to your own life script.

Dramatic people like to get and hold your attention, but if you delete them from the daily playbill and go on about your business, they have to find another source of attention. After all, it's the attention that keeps their drama working for them. It is hard to be the star of the play when no one is in your audience. It is equally hard to intentionally get up from your seat in the audience and walk out on the show. If you are going to be able to step out of other people's drama, you will have to leave it with Somebody far bigger than you. It is usually too hard to just turn around and walk away, leaving them alone on the stage.

It is important to let people know when you have put them in God's hands because when they realize you are not going to think or cover for them anymore, they begin to think for themselves or find someone else to think for them. You will have to summon the courage to make it clear that you take no responsibility for their future actions. That realization is pretty sobering for most people accustomed to having someone else carry their burdens.

Most of the time, letting go is a process. It takes a while to convince dependent loved ones that you have changed a long-term pattern of bailing them out. If you continue to hold firm and remain strong in your decision to release them, they will slowly begin to believe you. Before long, you will realize that your stress level is down because you will be living only one life—yours.

Hopefully, when you no longer participate in the drama, the one you have carried will become tired of their own burdens. That is the perfect place for them to face reality, and it is a wonderful place for you to be an example of doing life the right way. You can lead the way, because when you pressed the Delete button, you were practicing the ancient spiritual discipline of "casting all your care upon Him, for He cares for you" (1 Peter 5: 7 NKJV). The Greek word for *casting* means "to hurl." When you hurl something, you usually do not intend to get it back. Just as when you press Delete, it rarely is with the intention of seeing it again.

Drama du jour

Harriet's *drama du jour* was her teenage daughter, Britney, who was arrested and jailed for a DUI. That was not the first drama.

Britney had been drinking for several years, as well as taking drugs. She also had managed to flunk out of school.

Harriet called her friend, who happened to be a Christian life coach, in a totally distraught state. She was calling to ask if the coach thought she should bail Britney out of jail.

The coach asked several questions. (It pays to have friends who are life coaches.) "What do you think Britney will learn if you take her out of jail?"

Harriet's push back was, "What do you think will happen to her in there if I don't?"

The coach and Harriet agreed there were risks on both sides of the question. The coach, however, was wise enough to know that Harriet had to find her own answer and take responsibility for her decision.

They opened the Scriptures together to 1 Peter 5:6–7 in the Amplified Bible. (Just like a coach to want it spelled out in as many words as possible!)

Therefore humble yourselves [demote, lower yourselves in your own estimation] under the mighty hand of God, that in due time He may exalt you, casting the whole of your care [all your anxieties, all your worries, all your concerns, once and for all] on Him, for He cares for you affectionately and cares about you watchfully.

Harriet asked for specifics. "How do you 'cast a care'?" she asked. All she really wanted at that point was a fast answer to her question about leaving her daughter in jail. The coach knew she had to become quiet and get her answer directly from God in order to offer a place of peace. The coach also knew Harriet needed some very concrete directions, so she suggested that Harriet go home, get out a box, place a picture of Britney in it, along with some items that represented her childhood. Next, she encouraged her to write a prayer for Britney, listing God's promises to her. Then she was to put the box in a prominent place in her bedroom. That place would represent an altar. Then the coach asked Harriet to pray and surrender her daughter to God's will.

Harriet found a box, did what was suggested, and chose a cedar chest that was at the foot of her bed to be her altar. She knelt there and cast her anxiety on God, surrendering her daughter into His will. By the time she had done what she was asked, she was calm. Writing the promises had helped her focus beyond her immediate dilemma. She began to receive faith from God Himself, faith that He heard her prayers for Britney's well-being, as well as her prayer from a mother's heart for guidance.

After her prayer of relinquishment, she decided she would leave Britney in jail overnight and see what happened. She chose to move one step at a time. She would reevaluate in the morning. The next morning, Harriet was grateful to hear that nothing bad had happened during Britney's night in jail and that she would be released the next day, pending a court hearing.

Her story with Britney continues, but Harriet has her box, and it is a reminder that Britney is in God's care. She has cast that care on Him. It is not hers to take up again. Britney's drama is not going to consume Harriet's whole life. She is writing a new story in her relationship with her daughter. Harriet is Harriet and has her own story to write. Britney is her daughter, but she has another story to write, and she will not be the star in Harriet's *drama du jour*.

Hannah

We have a sweet sister in the Scriptures who understood the tensions and complications of an intense drama in her life. It is one most of us would recognize as highly uncomfortable and difficult. It is the drama of infertility in the presence of the fertile "other woman."

> Now there was a certain man of Ramathaim Zophim, of the mountains of Ephraim, and his name was Elkanah . . . And he had two wives: the name of one was Hannah, and the name of the other Peninnah. Peninnah had children, but Hannah had no children.
>
> This man went up from his city yearly to worship and sacrifice to the LORD of hosts in Shiloh . . . And whenever the time came for Elkanah to make an offering, he would give portions to Peninnah his wife and to all her sons and daughters. But to Hannah he would give a double portion, for he loved Hannah, although the LORD had closed her womb. And her rival also provoked her severely, to make her miserable, because the LORD had closed her womb. So it was, year by year, when she went up to the house of the LORD, that she provoked her; therefore she wept and did not eat. (1 Sam. 1:1–7 NKJV)

Uh-oh. Not only is the other woman in the house fertile, but she has a nasty attitude and a ritual. Go to the house of the Lord and provoke Hannah. A drama queen and an untenable situation.

Stop and think about the drama queens you know. How do they play out their stories? Are you dealing with one right now?

What kind of trouble does she engender, and how often does she do it? This is just food for thought for this moment, not for ongoing rumination. There is no point in that. The main thought to take away is that drama queens carry drama with them wherever they go, and they can be expected to perform on cue. The other point to keep in mind is that you do not have to participate. There is a definite pivotal step you can make to turn away from the theater.

When you turn *from* the *drama du jour*, it takes practice to know what to turn *toward* in order to write a new story in your life. When there is so much drama and emotional engagement, it is hard to bear the silence and really see what the day holds. It usually is not in the activity but in the quiet moments of looking and listening that clarity comes.

It probably will take tweaking some old attitudes to embrace each day for its intrinsic value—a day you can choose to approach with a generous spirit. Fewer months left on your life calendar may make you aware of the gift of days, but even if you have more potential days left than you have already lived, embracing the days and recognizing their value will change the tenor of your story.

Flashes of Paradise

Eve lived in Paradise. That was her original story, but she did not embrace it. She believed the deceiver's lie that "God is holding out on you" and "God doesn't mean what He says." Consequently she lost Paradise and had to live a different story. Don't you know that for the rest of her life there were days when she had flashes of Paradise? There were times when she passed a flowering bush or a singing brook and remembered the beauty of her days in the Garden of Eden?

God has provided flashes of paradise for each of us as we walk through our lives. We may not see the whole picture He paints for us because, like Eve, our vision is blocked by the drama of our own story or someone else's, but we can catch glimpses of paradise and embrace them. Each day provides its own beauty because we are alive.

Snow has just started to fall here at my home in Tennessee as I'm writing this. In the quiet I am looking out my office window, watching birds gather around the feeders to stock up for the frigid duration. Like all the people flocking to grocery stores for bread, milk, and bananas, the birds gather their seed to prepare for the coming cold, icy night. They are beautiful in their feathery coats of many colors and highly vocal in their multiple songs.

I am sitting in the quiet of my house, watching, wanting to take it all in, to step into the edge of their world for just a moment. And I remember the words of Jesus: "Are not five sparrows sold for two pennies? Yet not one of them is forgotten by God" (Luke 12:6 NIV). If there were drama going on in my world, how could I live in the *now* of this moment? How could I have time to focus? How could I listen and maybe hear whispers from eternity or see flashes of paradise? I couldn't.

Several months ago I was speaking at a conference. I was listening to the music, standing on the front row with my head bowed. I was absorbing the music and enjoying the empty space around me. At that moment a set of stairs appeared in my mind, and at the top was Jesus with a red robe draped around Him. He was looking back over His shoulder with eyes of such love and compassion that I almost gasped. I gazed at Him for another minute, and then I had to open my eyes and walk up on the podium to speak.

That was a flash of paradise. I have not forgotten that moment. I still can see Him, looking over His shoulder. I will never forget His face. It has come back to me many times since that day. It was a time of quiet in a place without drama, where God allowed my mind's eye to catch a glimpse of the majesty of His Son. If my head had been full of drama—mine or anyone else's—I could not have experienced that precious moment. That is a time and place filed away in my personal story, a moment without the interference of old stuff. I believe God is more than willing to give us these glimpses of eternity—those memories of paradise—that can be part of our ongoing transition from one period of our lives to another.

Being present in the *now* is an art. It makes today important without the baggage of yesterday and the angst of tomorrow. It becomes an art form that requires practice, but the more you are aware of the moment, the more you can drink in the essence of today. Life is going to happen, whether you pay attention or not. You are living a story, whether you recognize it or not. And you are writing a story, whether you want to or not. We live in the *now*, and until tomorrow comes, we are not there. Life is *today*. Leaving behind the *drama du jour* gives us a chance to move to a less cluttered life. It is all about the choices you make. God has a big story that includes you, but it is up to you whether you will live it out. It is your choice to write your lesser story by paying attention to the uncluttered *now* in which you live.

If you are alive, you will encounter drama. It always is amazing how stories that start out very simply can become huge, front-page news very quickly. A small town near here has been the backdrop for a major court battle between a teacher and three parents who claim that she molested their children. It has been heart wrenching to see the drama played out on the news, first locally and then nationally.

> *Yes, life is a whole string of nows knit together with friendship and songs, heartaches and tears, fears and courage, passion and compassion, depression and elation, patience and impatience, and more . . . So don't miss life. Take up your life and walk, whether it's happy or sad, angry or disappointing, ecstatic, hopeful, heart wrenching or tender. You name it! Just don't miss it. It is your gift to unwrap as you move through the hours. It is God offering hospitality to you as you move into tomorrow.[1]*
>
> —Macrina Wiederkehr

The teacher won the court battle and was declared not guilty on twenty-two counts, but she will forever live with the notoriety of the trial. An even bigger war rages now as she tries to regain custody of her own children. I am sure no one in this case ever dreamed that his or her life would be swept up in such a major drama. They all are forever changed and forever living stories they never set out to write. Something went wrong somewhere, and the simplicity of normal relationships turned into a horrible dramatic tragedy out of control. None of them can reclaim the days that have been lost. None of them will ever view life with the same innocence they once embraced.

Being present in the now is an art. It makes today important without the baggage of yesterday and the angst of tomorrow.

If they are wise, they will move on, but their stories have been forever rewritten in ways they never would have chosen. It happens sometimes. That is why God has to be the ultimate arbiter and final storyteller in our lives.

A Modern Old Story

As we have seen, Hannah was dealing with issues of infertility and depression while her husband had children with another wife. Sounds strikingly modern, doesn't it? But watch as Hannah succeeds in disengaging from her drama queen, Peninnah, and begins writing a new story:

> Peninnah would tease Hannah and upset her, because the LORD had made her unable to have children. This happened every year when they went up to the house of the LORD at Shiloh. Peninnah would upset Hannah until Hannah would cry and not eat anything. Her husband Elkanah would say to her, "Hannah, why are you crying and why won't you eat? Why are you sad? Don't I mean more to you than ten sons?" (1 Sam. 1:6–8)

Oh, please, Elkanah! It is not all about *you*. You are one sweet guy, but no, you don't mean more to Hannah "than ten sons." Elkanah seemed to be sympathetic but naive about what was going on with his wives! So Hannah took her case to a Higher Court: "She made a promise, saying, 'LORD ALL-POWERFUL, see how sad I am. Remember me and don't forget me. If you will give me a son, I will give him back to you all his life, and no one will ever cut his hair with a razor'" (v. 11).

Hannah was pouring out her heart to God, and Eli was watching her mouth. He thought she was drunk because her lips were moving, but he could not hear her saying anything. The next thing Hannah knew, Eli was telling her to stop getting drunk and to throw away her wine. Hannah defended herself, telling the old priest that she was not drunk, but she was just deeply troubled. Defending herself seemed to be her main pastime.

Imagine Hannah's distress. Her husband loved her but was clueless to her deep hurt. She went to the place where she should have been accepted and poured out her heart to the Lord, and the priest accused her of being drunk. Talk about piling on! She must have thought, *I am living in such a crummy story.* At least, that is what some of us would have thought, but old Eli finally got it, blessed her, and sent her on her way.

Did you notice how Hannah's behavior and countenance changed after she brought her concerns to God?

> Early the next morning Elkanah's family got up and worshiped the LORD. Then they went back home to Ramah. Elkanah had sexual relations with his wife Hannah, and the LORD remembered her. So Hannah became pregnant, and in time she gave birth to a son. She named him Samuel, saying, "His name is Samuel because I asked the LORD for him." (vv. 19–20)

Hannah had the child she prayed for, and because she promised, the day came to take him to live at Shiloh, the center of their worship of God. Talk about a circuitous story! You ask God, you receive what you asked, and you give it back to God, an interesting model to consider, and Hannah is an excellent example:

> When Samuel was old enough to eat, Hannah took him to the house of the LORD at Shiloh, along with a three-year-old bull, one-half bushel of flour, and a leather bag filled with wine. After they had killed the bull for the sacrifice, Hannah brought Samuel to Eli. She said to Eli, "As surely as you live, sir, I am the same woman who stood near you praying to the LORD. I prayed for this child, and the LORD answered my prayer and gave him to me. Now I give him back to the LORD. He will belong to the LORD all his life." And he worshiped the LORD there. (vv. 24–28)

Samuel—Judge, Priest, Servant, Writer

The Bible records that Hannah's son, Samuel—the answer to her heartfelt prayer to God—excelled in his service to God. He was judge, priest, and humble servant, so God called Samuel on various occasions to perform important tasks. For instance, he anointed both Saul and David as kings over Israel. He led God's people faithfully and right throughout his life, always observing the Passover (2 Chron. 35:18). And he recorded the events of the life of King David: "Everything David did as king, from beginning to end, is recorded in the records of Samuel the seer" (1 Chron. 29:29).

Samuel was, in every way, an outstanding and faithful leader of God's people. And he was the first chapter in Hannah's new story because she had deleted the drama from her life, changed her attitude, and asked God to help her. What more is there to say?

Personal Reflection

1. Hard situations can quickly turn into drama if we are not careful to guard our hearts, especially when difficult people are just waiting to provoke us as Peninnah did to Hannah. Do you have someone creating drama in your life at every turn? Describe.

2. Hannah deleted the drama from her story. How will you go about deleting the drama from your story?

3. What troubles have you *assumed* and are carrying around that you need to bring to God and leave in His care today?

4. You ask God for something important to you, you receive what you asked for, and then you give it back to God. Have you ever lived such a story? If you have, describe it.

5. If you haven't lived such a story, would you want to? Why or why not?

6. What part of Hannah's story can you use to write your own new story? Explain.

7. How do you think you will feel when you have put your troubles into the hands of the almighty God?

Journal Entry

To continue your new story, complete the following starter sentence in your personal journal. Then continue writing thoughts and feelings from your heart as long as you need to.

The constant drama in my life centers around _____ (who?), and I can begin to delete that destructive drama by . .

Group Discussion Questions

1. What are the basic facts of Hannah's family life? How many people were involved in the marriage?

2. What do you perceive her relationship to Elkanah was?

3. What was Hannah's view of God? What did she say about Him that shows she knew Him well?

4. How did Hannah's situation of infertility turn into high drama?

5. How do you think Peninnah saw herself in this situation?

6. What do you imagine Peninnah might have said to Hannah?

7. How long did this situation go on? Was it short-lived or long-term?

8. How did Hannah allow Peninnah's torture to affect her emotions and behavior?

9. How did Hannah describe her situation and emotional state to Eli?

10. What do you think Hannah thought about Elkanah's clumsy efforts to comfort her?

11. What would you have recommended to Elkanah if you were his marriage counselor? What about to Hannah?

12. How does our view of God affect our ability to live above the drama of circumstances and the drama queens (or kings) in our lives?

Chapter 6

FORGET THE WHAT-MIGHT-HAVE-BEENS

Think of life as a terminal illness, because, if you do, you will live it with joy and passion, as it ought to be lived.

—Anna Quindlen

Anna

Anna was widowed at a very young age,
yet she chose life for all her years.

LUKE 2:36–38

Like most young women, Anna probably had a Cinderella
fantasy in mind for her life—Prince Charming, children, wonderful family, love, laughter, and growing old together. And for
the first seven years of her married life, Anna was a princess.

Then, while Anna was still very young, and after only seven
happy years of marriage, her husband suddenly died, leaving his
young wife as a widow and alone. If that had been you, what
would have been your response?

Anna's response is not at all what you would expect from
a young woman left alone in the world to survive on her own.
Instead of reacting with anger, bitterness, and angst, Anna
picked up her skirt and got back on the road of life. And you just
won't believe what she did for the rest of her life!

W hat-might-have-been does not exist, so don't even go there. For many years that has been my mantra. The words came to me one day as I sat at my computer writing phrases and verses that had gotten me through life thus far. As I rolled them around in my head, I thought about the what-might-have-beens that have bothered me during my life. They all are part of a tale that was never written and can never *be* written, so they are basically without form and baseless, but they have an odd way of cropping up from time to time, leaving a bubble of discontentment floating around in my thoughts. Do you recognize the thoughts in your own life that have that niggling, annoying way of pushing their way into your mind?

One of the what-might-have-beens that bothered me for years was the absence of a sibling. All my growing up years, I wished that—some way, somehow—I could have a brother or sister. I named my favorite doll "Brother" in hopes that someday, like Pinocchio, he would become a "real live boy." It never happened, of course, and the whole thought faded into the background as I grew up, married, and had my own children—all males, all brothers!

I was pretty content with the way things stood until my parents' health began to fail, and I became the one to rush to the hospital or to sit with them through the interminable hours of waiting that illness brings. I hated having the whole thing on my shoulders. I often thought, *I wish there were someone else to help bear this burden. I wish I had a brother or sister to talk to about this.*

Some of you are reading this and laughing, saying, "Crazy girl, you should know *my* brother. Be glad you didn't have to deal with *him* when you were under pressure! I've had to carry everything alone although he is alive and well and living just across town." I hear you, and maybe your what-might-have-been is a brother who felt the same responsibility you did. I understand, but you catch my gist. We all have what-might-have-beens that bubble up out of our discontentment. We wish things had been different, and "if only" they had, we are convinced life would have been better, and our stories would have been different.

What if God had made you taller? What if God had made you smaller? What if God had made you a blonde? What if God had made you lean and tan? What if God had made you white? Black? Rich? Brilliant? What if God had given you a great voice for singing? What if you had married someone different? Had a son? A daughter? What if your daddy had not been a drunk? Your mother had said, "I love you"? Your brother had not come into your room that night? What if the water had been deeper when you dived into that pool headfirst? What if the girls in the dorm had not lied about you? What if you had said no to your first boyfriend? Said no to getting rid of your baby? Had thought about STDs? Taken AIDS seriously? What if you had been a more involved mom? What if you had paid more attention to your teenage daughter? Or talked to your son about drugs? What if you had told your children more about the Lord while they would still listen? *What if, what if, what if?* The questions go on and on, and the more you entertain them, the less contentment you have.

Reality check: what is, *is*! And it's the what-is in your life that allows you to write a new story. You can find the contentment of accepting what is and writing about it, rather than sitting in the despondency of what-might-have-been. Life changes, and our old stories can become laments for our losses. Writing a new story creates a new normal. The nest empties, a spouse retires, finances become more limited, a parent requires more attention, grandchildren grow up and do not come around, or a lifelong friend dies or leaves town. These are all changes we must face at times.

The Secret of Contentment

There is a dear woman named Anna in the Scriptures we often overlook, but her story is one of learning to become content with herself. She arrived just as Jesus' parents brought Him to the temple on the eighth day after His birth.

> There was also a prophetess, Anna, the daughter of Phanuel, of the tribe of Asher. She was very old; she had lived with her husband seven years after her marriage, and then was a widow until she was eighty-four. She never left the temple but worshiped night and day, fasting and praying. Coming up to them at that very moment, she gave thanks to God and spoke about the child to all who were looking forward to the redemption of Jerusalem. (Luke 2:36–38 NIV)

Anna found a new story. When we meet her in Luke 2, she was eighty-four years old. No children are mentioned. So we do not know if she had children or not, but we do know that she found a new story as a worshipper of God, *never leaving the temple.* Imagine! The other clue we have about her is that she was disciplined. She prayed, fasted, and obviously had listened carefully to the rabbi when he taught from the Torah because she was looking for the redemption of Israel.

She had not spent her life alone rehearsing what-might-have-been. She had found her place of service in the safest place she knew, the temple of God. She had found contentment. And she treasured it.

Learning the secret of contentment is another one of those easier-said-than-done art forms, but when you prioritize it in your thinking and in your self-talk, you find you are living in a new story—a story where you soothe yourself with contentment on all levels. The options for reactions are many, and they are all up to us. But the choice to learn how to content ourselves is a blessing we may not begin to understand until we write the story. Until you have seen someone wrestle with what-might-have-been and lose, you have no idea what a gift the art of contenting yourself can be.

I believe learning to content yourself begins with the acknowledgment that God is God, and you are not. That means He is in control. You cannot read through the Scriptures and understand God's story without recognizing that He calls the shots. He reigns. Humanity has always fought with that idea because it is hard for us to bow to the fact that an unseen hand holds our lives, and whether good or bad is happening, He is in control of it all. In Isaiah 45:5–7, He writes this:

> *I am the LORD. There is no other God;*
> *I am the only God.*
> *I will make you strong,*
> *even though you don't know me,*

SAME LIFE, NEW STORY

so that everyone will know
there is no other God.
From the east to the west they will know
I alone am the Lord.
I made the light and the darkness.
I bring peace, and I cause troubles.
I, the Lord, *do all these things.*

Our questions kick in, and often we begin to ask, "But what about *this*? Can *this* be under His control? Did He really allow *that*? Is He really good enough to be trusted? Why did He not do things differently? Why am I dealing with this pain? Why does He not do something about this awful situation?"

You can only write a brand-new story, leaving out the past stains of doubt and hurt, if you make the decision that God is in control, and you are not going to fight with Him. He continues this way:

> *Learning to content yourself begins with the acknowledgment that God is God, and you are not.*

Woe to him who quarrels with his Maker,
to him who is but a potsherd among the potsherds on
the ground.
Does the clay say to the potter,
"What are you making?"
Does your work say,
"He has no hands?"
This is what the Lord *says—*
the Holy One of Israel, and its Maker:
Concerning things to come,

do you question me about my children,
or give me orders about the work of my hands?
It is I who made the earth
and created mankind upon it.
My own hands stretched out the heavens;
I marshaled their starry hosts. (vv. 9, 11–12 NIV)

A Quarrel with the Maker

"Quarreling with your Maker" is a useless exercise in frustration. I have watched many women find themselves in a quarrel they did not want but they do not seem to be able to lay down. One in particular had so much going for her. She is talented and beautiful, but the career she had dreamed of all her life never came to fruition. She had always had hopes of being a writer. She was in her early forties when she began to fight with the realities of a life that was not working as she wanted. Just about the time she was looking for her longed-for career to take off, it fell apart in front of her eyes. She kept looking for a way to revive it, but it appeared to be completely dead. Nothing was the way she had dreamed it.

Every book project was rejected, and although she had opportunity to speak occasionally, it never was enough. She knew she had something to say, but she just never found a place to say it. The pain of that, plus her own doubts and questions about God, took her down a path of wondering, *Is He good? Does He care? Does He have my best interest in mind?* Her journey proved her belief that God was somehow more interested in causing her pain than in being on her side.

As the years passed, her life was plagued with losses. Her

extended family is a continuing saga of broken relationships and struggles. Her health understandably took a turn for the worse. The problem was never clearly pinpointed, but she always felt bad. (You cannot quarrel with God and stay healthy. Our bodies were not meant to be in that fight.) The message she so wanted to write lay crumpled at her feet. She's had to face the fact that she may have been holding on to a dream that was not hers to dream. It was hard and humbling because she never had seen herself doing anything else. Everyone had told her she was so good at writing. She believed it and held on, waiting for God to show up in a big way. To her way of thinking, He never came.

You cannot fight with God and win.

She finally had to admit it: she has a quarrel with her Maker. Life has not turned out the way she wanted. To her, God seems too far away and disinterested. At other times, He seems much too close, thwarting anything she tries. Her story has many chapters, but they are all about the same thing—what-might-have-been. She has honest questions that need to be answered before she can move on, though I often wonder, does she really want answers? Would she be content with them if they were not what she expected? I don't know. I just know it is a treacherous thing to quarrel with your Maker.

Writing a new story when the circumstances have not changed is hard. We cannot go back and undo the events of the past. It is possible, however, to dare to turn the page and to begin putting a few new phrases on the first line. Thoughts like, *I give up the fight,* or *My quarrel is not with my Maker,* or *I want to rehearse the good things He has done for me,* will turn the tide of your story. You cannot fight with God and win. You cannot continue being angry with God and expect that your war with Him will change your circumstances.

Lecturing God with "You *should* have" and "You *could* have" leaves you in a precarious position, at odds with the One who holds your breath in His hand. He is big enough to listen to that from us, but does He really deserve it? He is the One who has plans for us, and when we can relax and know that His plans are for good and not for evil (Jer. 29:11), we can begin to write a new story full of hope and wonder at all that He *has done* and *will do* in our lives.

Questions from God

Our old friend Job, husband of Mrs. Job—who counseled him to curse God and die—is a picture of a human caught in the dark of what-might-have-been. His life had been turned upside down, his friends had turned against him, and he seemed to be trying to hang on to his reason about God's dealings with him. Enter God, who unleashes an incredible soliloquy of reason that Job could not deny. Neither could you nor I, if God sat us down to explain some things. God says this to Job:

> Who is this that questions my wisdom with such ignorant words? Brace yourself like a man, because I have some questions for you and you must answer them.
>
> Where were you when I laid the foundations of the earth? Tell me, if you know so much . . . Who kept the sea inside its boundaries as it burst from the womb, and as I clothed it with clouds and wrapped it in thick darkness? For I locked it behind

barred gates, limiting its shores. I said, "This far and no farther will you come. Here your proud waves must stop!"

Have you ever commanded the morning to appear and caused the dawn to rise in the east? Have you made daylight spread to the ends of the earth to bring an end to the night's wickedness? . . .

Have you explored the springs from which the seas come? Have you explored their depths?

Do you know where the gates of death are located? Have you seen the gates of utter gloom?

Do you realize the extent of the earth? Tell me about it if you know! (Job 38:2–4, 8–13, 16–18 NLT)

The first move toward contenting yourself is to agree with the fact that God is God, and you are not! That puts you and God in two different categories. On the one hand, God has the big picture in mind, operates from His eternal perspective and from His heart of lovingkindness, doing what is best for us in the long run. We, on the other hand, operate from our *memories* and our *current* awareness. We cannot know the *tomorrows*, so how can we argue with the One who has already lived there in His ever-present (omnipresent), all-knowing (omniscient), all-powerful (omnipotent) state? He knows what is *going* to happen and somehow, through all of the mystery, makes us a promise that we can stand on with confidence:

We are assured and know that [God being a partner in their labor] all things work together and are [fitting into a plan] for good to and for those who love God and are called according to [His] design and purpose.

For those whom He foreknew [of whom He was aware and loved beforehand], He also destined from the beginning [foreordaining them] to be molded into the image of His Son [and share inwardly His likeness], that He might become the firstborn among many brethren. (Rom. 8:28–29 AMP)

What a gift! We do not have to make all the different paragraphs and chapters in our stories make sense in order for them to work for good in God's plan. God is constantly doing things behind the scenes in our backstories. He promises that *all things* will be made to work for good for those who love Him and are called according to His design and purpose. By the way, you do not have to worry because if you love Him, you *are* called. The Bible makes it clear: "We love because God first loved us" (1 John 4:19). So He puts the will to love Him in our hearts as part of our call to be molded into the image of His Son. That might feel like a big theological chunk to swallow when you are just looking for a way to content yourself in your circumstances. I understand, but I have learned that knowing what God says is the best antidote for our propensity to talk to ourselves about the hard, unexplainable things that happen in life.

Rehearse Your Blessings

The second major step toward writing a new story of contenting yourself is to rehearse your blessings. It is easy to focus on the hard things and disappointments, and it is easy to blame God for what seems wrong. Sadly, that leaves you out in the cold with a story that has no hope or redemption. Contentment comes from learning a secret, a secret that requires you to have some experience at both *having* what you want and *not having* what you want. The apostle Paul wrote the following words to some people who had sent him an offering. He was grateful, but in his heart he knew that whether anyone saw to his needs or not, he would be fine. That had come from experience!

> Not that I speak from want, for I have learned to be content in whatever circumstances I am. I know how to get along with humble means, and I also know how to live in prosperity; in any and every circumstance I have learned the secret of being filled and going hungry, both of having abundance and suffering need. I can do all things through Him who strengthens me. (Phil. 4:11–13 NASB)

In this same letter, Paul told the readers to "be anxious for nothing" (4:6 NASB) and to think about good things (4:8) if they wanted to have a peace that passes understanding (4:7). Clearly, he had written some chapters in his story, and he had learned some things about being content. Were those lessons always easy? Not at all! But they paid off for Paul in the long run.

You and I can learn some things from our own stories. They are simple truths that will take us to the next story with more hope and optimism and, above all, contentment! We can learn to content ourselves when we remember these axioms:

- Forget the what-might-have-beens. They do not exist.
- Don't go to war with your Maker. He is God, and you are not.

- Rehearse your blessings. Every life has good things. Look at the good things. Relish them, rehearse them, remember them!

Writing a new story of contenting yourself will not require a lot of deep digging. It just means you will relax into the what-is instead of always scrambling for the what-I-want.

Trapped in What-Is

My mother's end-of-life experience was one that would have been a challenge to anyone. At age eighty-seven she broke her hip, but it did not heal after surgery. She was bedridden and lived her life in one room, either in a bed or a chair. She had caregivers who brought her every meal, bathed her, fixed her hair, and took care of all her personal needs. She went from being a very active, social older woman to an invalid spending unending hours in a hospital bed or recliner.

Her mind was clear and creative, but her body had shut down on her. She was trapped by what-is.

Many people commented that they would not be able to stand her life of confinement if they were in her situation. I admit, looking at the way she lived, I would have thought the same thing. But because I was her daughter and spent so much time with her, I saw that she had learned the secret of contenting herself, and amazingly it did not depend on other people making her happy.

She worked on a laptop computer, had an iPod, and loved her little cell phone that stayed by her bed. She read voraciously, keeping a meticulous list of every book she completed.

She listened to hours on end of Bill and Gloria Gaither videos. (God bless the Gaithers for this gift to people who are homebound!)

She studied her Bible in order to teach a little weekly class of women her age who gathered in the great room outside her door. Her caregiver used the sling designed to transport invalids from one place to another and would seat her on her little wheeled chair that she could drive, sort of, and out she would go to teach. She always wore earrings and a pretty top for that event. She taught with confidence and authority, although much of her audience was deaf as was she! Their responses, though mostly unheard by my mother, were met with her delighted smile. She had learned a secret. She contented herself with where she was.

The last week of her life was spent in a hospital room. She was suffering from a raging infection that had attacked her kidneys, but even in that situation, she contented herself. She liked her room, she liked the nurses, and she even liked the notoriously bad hospital food!

The day Mother died, her brother and sisters were by her bedside singing hymns with her. They reminisced about the songs they had loved as children and sang them with her in her final hours on earth.

As the afternoon began to wane and the dark of evening was coming on, her condition worsened, and her body began to shut down completely. No medicine was going to save her. She had lived eighty-nine years and ten months.

Mother did not make the ninetieth birthday celebration we had planned for her, and I did not make it to her bedside when she died. Days before, she had assured me that she was fine and said, "Go on to your conference." I had no idea I would never see her on this earth again. We had been through many hospital visits and close calls before, so I left, believing that, as every other time, she would bounce back and I would see her in a few days. The next time I saw her was in her casket.

I had wanted to be there, but "what-might-have-been does not exist," so I knew not to let my emotions settle into the what-ifs. God could have kept her alive until I got to her bedside, but I knew not to argue with my Maker. He knows best. There were blessings to be counted, and I knew it, so I got about doing the only thing I knew to do—being grateful for the many good things I could number in the middle of my loss.

I needed to content myself as I had seen my mother do many times during her last three years. One of her favorite phrases when asked, "How are you doing?" was "I could complain, but I won't." So with her words in mind, I chose not to complain but to find every good thing I could in the midst of loss and sorrow.

It was not long until her caregiver, Grace, came to me and asked me if I wanted to know what Mother's passing had been like. I said yes, and Grace described a scene that had many sad and good things about it. The most important one to me was the last words Mother spoke: "Thank You, Lord, for taking care of me all of my life. Thank You, Lord, for being so good to me." Then, with one last wave of her arm toward heaven, she said, "I see, I see . . ." She was content to be going home at last.

I am content to begin a new story—a story without my mother, a new story that never will include the brother who did not exist, and a new story full of memories and blessings too numerous to recall!

Anna's Choice

While you think about contenting yourself in your own story, let's go back and revisit Anna, the dear old lady who lived in the temple for so many years. For a woman who lived so long, Anna's story is captured in startlingly few words by Luke in his gospel account. After losing her husband to death early in marriage, Anna lived a life of contentment, and before the end of her life, she got to see the Christ child with her own eyes.

Clearly Anna made a choice about how she would live a life she could never have anticipated. Before we look at Anna's story, we will start a little earlier in the chapter to help us see the backstory, which makes it easier to understand the bigger story being told.

At that time, Augustus Caesar sent an order that all people in the countries under Roman rule must list their names in a register. This was the first registration; it was taken while Quirinius was governor of Syria. And all went to their own towns to be registered.

So Joseph left Nazareth, a town in Galilee, and went to the town of Bethlehem in Judea, known as the town of David. Joseph went there because he was from the family of David. Joseph registered with Mary, to whom he was engaged and who was now pregnant. While they were in Bethlehem, the time came for Mary to have the baby, and she gave birth to her first son. Because there were no rooms left in the inn, she wrapped the baby with pieces of cloth and laid him in a feeding trough . . .

When the baby was eight days old, he was circumcised

and was named Jesus, the name given by the angel before the baby began to grow inside Mary.

When the time came for Mary and Joseph to do what the law of Moses taught about being made pure, they took Jesus to Jerusalem to present him to the Lord. (It is written in the law of the Lord: "Every firstborn male shall be given to the Lord.") Mary and Joseph also went to offer a sacrifice, as the law of the Lord says: "You must sacrifice two doves or two young pigeons." (Luke 2:1–7, 21–24)

Now let's look at Luke 2:36–38 again and see how the backstory relates to Anna:

There was also a prophetess, Anna, the daughter of Phanuel, of the tribe of Asher. She was very old; she had lived with her husband seven years after her marriage, and then was a widow until she was eighty-four. She never left the temple but worshiped night and day, fasting and praying. Coming up to them at that very moment, she gave thanks to God and spoke about the child to all who were looking forward to the redemption of Jerusalem. (NIV)

What do we learn about Anna's family situation? (Just a little side note: Anna was from the tribe of Asher, and Asher was one of Leah's sons, whose name means "happy.") Luke 6:45 says, "Good people bring good things out of the good they stored in their hearts. But evil people bring evil things out of the evil they stored in their hearts. People speak the things that are in their hearts." Notice what Jesus says about the connection between the heart and the mouth.

Old Story, New Story

In truth, Anna's old story had all the ingredients needed to make her into a cranky old woman. She could have succumbed to bitterness and sorrow after the death of her husband. She could have reveled in loneliness and despair. She could have blamed God for her troubles. In other words, she could have reacted just as many of us would. Instead, Anna wrote a new story of contentment in service and passion for God that will continue to be told throughout history, influencing millions of people for good.

As is often true, without her old story to set the stage, Anna would have had no reason to write a new story of dedication to her God and contentment with her life of service. Old stories always precede new stories. So whatever old story you are living now may well be the introduction to a grand new story just around the corner.

Personal Reflection

1. Describe one area of what-might-have-been in your own life and how you are dealing with it today.
2. Do you find yourself kicking against what *is* and wishing things could be different? Give a specific example.
3. If you had been in Anna's place, do you think you would have responded the same way she did? Why or why not?
4. If you had lived in the temple for so many years, how do you think you would have felt actually to see the Christ child as she did? Describe what you think those feelings would be in detail.
5. What do you believe God's plan is for your life? Describe.
6. Do you think you are sincerely trying to follow God's plan, or are you resisting His plan for your life? Explain.
7. What can you apply this week from the life of Anna to help you live contented in the life God has blessed you with?
8. What blessings will you choose to rehearse this week?

Journal Entry

To continue your new story, complete the following starter sentence in your personal journal. Then continue writing thoughts and feelings from your heart as long as you need to.

The biggest what-might-have-been in my life that I need to eliminate is . . .

Group Discussion Questions

1. What opportunities do the circumstances of Anna's life give her for bitterness or angst? Why?

2. Describe a time of what-might-have-been in your life, and how have you dealt with it? (Wait for volunteers to answer.)

3. What is the problem with what-might-have-beens? And what should we do with them?

4. Do you ever say or wonder what-if about something in your life? Who would be willing to share an example? (Wait for volunteers to answer.)

5. How did Anna choose to live in response to her life alone for so many years?

6. What consumed Anna's life? And how does that compare to the way most people respond to life's struggles?

7. What comes out of Anna's mouth when she sees the Christ child?

8. What lessons can we draw from Anna's life and example to apply to our own lives?

9. Do you believe that God has a specific plan for your life? Who would be willing to share that with us?

10. How can we begin to eliminate the what-might-have-beens and what-ifs from our lives?

Chapter 7

DISCOVER THE POWER OF WISDOM AND COURAGE COMBINED

I will utter dark sayings of old, which . . . our fathers have told us. We will not hide them from their children, telling to the generation to come . . .

—Psalm 78:2–4 NKJV

Jehosheba

Jehosheba could have played it safe, but she
wisely risked saving a child and a kingdom.

2 CHRONICLES 22:11–12

Talk about drama! King Ahaziah was murdered. So the
wicked Queen Mother, Athaliah, killed the rest of the
royal family so she could rule the country. That is, she
killed everyone in the royal family except a baby boy named
Joash—her dead son's son, her grandson. And the only reason
she did not kill him was because his Aunt Jehosheba, princess
and Ahaziah's sister, kidnapped him and hid him from the evil
queen.

In fact, Jehosheba hid Joash and his nurse for the next six
long years while Athaliah ruled! And where did she hide them?
In the temple of the Lord! Who would think to look there for a
tiny fugitive from the queen?

Wisdom and courage joined forces when Jehosheba took
action to save the future king of Judah. And the long-term results
for her and an entire nation are amazing!

K ate MacRae was five years old when the tremor that started in her hand sent her and her mother to the pediatrician's office. Thinking that there would be a simple answer and that they would be home with the rest of the family for dinner that night, they walked into the office totally unaware of the wisdom and courage that would have to combine in the battle for Kate's life.

Shockingly, Kate was sent to the hospital and soon diagnosed with an aggressive, involved brain tumor that was invading her brain without mercy. She and her family were thrown into a world about which they had no knowledge—the frightening world of pediatric cancer. They came face-to-face with facts young parents never think they will have to encounter with a five-year-old: brain surgery, paralysis, brutal rounds of chemo, death in the next room, vomiting that would not stop, exhaustion beyond remedy, and a future that could be shut down at any given moment. Circumstances dropped on their lives like planes hitting towers, hurricanes hitting cities, and earthquakes decimating populations. Their whole world was rocked.

Kate's mom, Holly, began to blog their journey from day one. She spoke with transparency and gutsiness that only comes from deep within when the stakes are incredibly high and the choices have dwindled to a precious few. Like Job of old, Holly declared through her agony, "Though He slay me, yet will I trust Him" (Job 13:15 NKJV). Or as the New Century Version says it,

"Even if God kills me, I have hope in him; I will still defend my ways to his face."

Holly wrote this in her first entry:

We believe strongly in the power of prayer and the ability of Jesus to heal our precious daughter. Whether He does this through modern medicine or simply a divine touch, we aren't picky. We are asking others to join us on this journey and fervently pray for our Kate. The road is long and unbelievably hard. We have three children, all who are intensely affected. Olivia is now seven, Kate is five, and Will is four. Please keep all of us in your prayers as we try to walk this journey of childhood cancer.

Today, seven months later and into a very dangerous transplant phase, Holly still writes with courage and wisdom that she has called on every day:

Day 6 of transplant. Difficult emotionally. The morning was rough as we awoke to the news that Kate's kidney function continued to drop, so again the chemo was readjusted. Then it was on to fighting to get medications down, Kate crying and asking why I was being so mean, making her take her medications. How do you explain to a six-year-old how much you love her and that I would be momentarily "mean" to get a chance at a lifetime with her? I kept silent, a few tears falling. I wonder if that is what Jesus so often says?

People, such the following writer, read Holly's blog, pray, and stand in awe of a woman who faces even the impossible days with courage and wisdom:

I am praying harder this round than ever for Kate. It just sounds so much harder this time, especially with tomorrow's new drug. May I say, however, that for all of the blessings that I ask for your family, I feel that you are a blessing to me. You have helped me to realize how blessed I am, but you and Aaron [Kate's father] both also teach me something new with every entry. Not only are you advocating on Kate's behalf, not only is Kate touching everyone reading your blog, but you both do as well. I think that some people buckle and fall to their knees with devastating news like yours, but it's people like you who can change the world with your love of Christ and family and dedication, and accomplish so much. I appreciate your entries, and I really truly feel blessed to be able to follow Kate's story, and blessed to be able to pray for all of you. Thank you for giving us this opportunity.

—Danielle Tipton, FL (2/12/10)

God has taken Kate's story all over the world since Holly wrote that first blog. People of prayer have joined the MacRaes' journey. With more than 8 million hits on their Web site, thousands of prayers have been offered for Kate. You can read their story for yourself at prayforkate.com. You might want to become one of the people who stand with this woman of strength and courage.

Story Backdrops

We don't get to pick our life circumstances. They happen, whether we are just *doing life*, and they come on us, or we cause them ourselves. To be sure, circumstances are often the backdrops of our stories. They are the foundational facts. They are the realities we must weave into our lives. They follow us wherever we go. Sometimes they are cut-and-dried, and we know what to do, but more often we are called to summon our wisdom and courage to face an intricate maze of questions without answers and decisions without guarantees.

I have come to understand that wisdom without courage is only half enough. Wisdom has to hold hands with courage when the circumstances become dicey, and we are in the process of redirecting our lives. Wisdom is the gift of knowing what to do. Courage is the gift of having the guts to do it! That is a powerful combination.

Esther is one of the women in biblical history who stands out as a prime example of what it means to live in a story in which she never dreamed she would become the hero. Yet her wisdom and courage allowed her to be used by God to save her people from the wrath and evil schemes of Haman, an immoral man who plotted death for the entire Jewish nation.

Esther was an orphaned Jewish girl who, through an uncanny set of circumstances, found favor with King Xerxes of Persia and, amazingly, became his queen. Her cousin Mordecai, who had raised Esther from childhood, heard that Haman, one of the king's courtiers, had set out to destroy the Jews. Tragically, Xerxes was going along with Haman's wicked plan, not realizing his own beloved Esther was a Jewess and that it was her people he was unwittingly allowing to be murdered.

Mordecai got word to Esther that the treachery was going forward, and she knew she had to do something. She could not stand by without telling the king, and yet there was a royal law that no one could approach the king without permission. To do so would mean death. So she moved with the wisdom and courage she had. The Scriptures record this:

> Then Esther told them to reply to Mordecai,
>
> "Go, assemble all the Jews who are found in Susa, and fast for me; do not eat or drink for three days, night or day. I and my maidens also will fast in the same way. And thus I will go in to the king, which is not according to the law; and if I perish, I perish." (Est. 4:15–16 NASB)

The plot grew thicker while Esther moved forward with wisdom and courage. She could do no less than to try to save her people. She approached King Xerxes, and he received her. The awful plans of Haman were revealed, and the king supplemented his decree so the Jews could defend themselves. As a result it was Haman who would die and not the Jews. But Esther had no guarantees. She knew the wise thing she had to do, and she desperately needed the courage to do it. Her story and that of her people would have been written very differently if her fear had kept her from operating in the wisdom and courage she was given.

Wisdom is the gift of knowing what to do. Courage is the gift of having the guts to do it!

Shattered Dreams

Many people can say, "If I had not stepped out in the wisdom and courage I was given, there is no way I would have had the life I have today." I have known more than one woman in my years of life coaching who has discovered something unexpected in their own homes, and this has made them face facts they never dreamed they would have to face and handle situations they never imagined they would have to handle.

Penny (not her real name) is one of those women. Her life today is free and fulfilling, although she has come to her new story through great pain and sorrow. She had been married a little more than six years when she discovered Ryan's stack of pornographic videos. He had hidden them in the basement behind the ductwork for the heat and air conditioning in their home. She was not looking for anything in particular when she went to the basement to rearrange some boxes to make room for a piece of furniture she wanted to move down there. But when the corner of a black plastic box caught her eye behind the silver duct, she began to investigate. What was that? What was it doing there?

As she looked closer, her heart sank. *Is this Ryan's? What's wrong with him? What's wrong with our marriage?* Then she began to rationalize. They had bought the house from another couple three years before. *Maybe the videos belonged to Mr. Harris? Maybe he left them?* It made her sick to think about the kindly Tom Harris being into porn, but it was probably his. That calmed her for a while, but when she went into the laundry room and found a porn magazine under a pile of old work towels folded in the corner, her heart began to palpitate as she thought, *What if it is Ryan's stuff? What if his nights of sitting up and not coming to bed are being spent looking at this? What if I don't really know the man I married?*

This pornographic find sent Penny on a journey of self-discovery that changed her forever. She put the magazine back where she found it, back side up. The next week she found it under the towels, front cover up. She had left the videos where she found them, stacked neatly on top of one another. Two weeks later, she saw they had been rearranged, definitely changed from the way she had left them. Once again the familiar sinking feeling hit her. What was she to do? What *could* she do? What would Ryan do if she told him she knew? What did all of this mean for their lives? What was next?

Penny had learned to pray as a child, so she thought, *If I ever need God to tell me what to do, it is now.* She prayed a simple "God, help!" prayer, and thoughts of what to do came to her. She had been so absorbed in her work and what was going on with her job that she had paid little attention to Ryan's emotional absence and physical withdrawal. As she thought about it, it had been going on for their whole married life. As soon as they were married, he went emotionally missing, and for long periods of time he was physically absent. He was in the house, but as Penny thought about it, Ryan was not there many nights. She had just gone to sleep tired, thinking he would come to bed later. Until she found the videos and magazine, she had no idea that they were in trouble.

As she prayed, God put in her spirit, "There is more." Sad but determined to discover what was going on, she found big chunks of money missing from their mutual account. She then found a Visa bill for some lingerie she had never seen. Knowing she had to say something, she quietly and calmly started with the bill and worked her way to the videos in the basement. Ryan denied it all at first, but once he knew he had been caught, he then agreed to go to counseling with Penny.

That lasted for three sessions before he began making excuses for why he could not go. Then he refused to talk about it altogether. Eight weeks later he told Penny he wanted out of the marriage. He had never loved her, and he had a girlfriend. Penny was devastated, but once again armed with wisdom and courage, she sought out counsel for what to do next. She was beginning to see that she had been asleep at the wheel, and this crash had been inevitable.

Penny came to her senses, prayed for her marriage, continued in counseling, and over a period of time, grew into a wise and courageous woman. Ryan moved out three months after he made his announcement, and despite Penny's attempts to reconcile, he refused. He filed for divorce and never looked back. She was left with her hopes and dreams in shattered pieces around her.

Although that was the end of the story in which Penny thought she was living, she was still alive and had a choice to make: she could bail out of her life and see herself as tarnished goods, or she could begin a new life. Had she failed to face the facts in front of her with courage and wisdom, she would likely still be living a lie and hoping Ryan would come to his senses and turn around.

How many women I know are living in that state! That is why I am passionate to say, "Wisdom and courage are available; use them!" You do not have to keep living the same old life, doing the same old things, but expecting the story to change. It won't. As the old adage says, "If you always do what you've always done, you'll always get what you've always had."

Robert Louis Stevenson once said, "I hate to write, but I love to have written." And that is usually true for us as well. The new story that requires courage and wisdom often is not one we planned or wanted to write, but the circumstances demand it. Usually we do not want to write such a new tale because the challenges that come with this kind of scenario are huge.

Interestingly, however, in God's big-story perspective, it is exactly in those situations where He does His most amazing work. The things you never dreamed you could do, you are able to do. The things you always said you could *not* do, somehow you *do*, and the glory of it all goes to God. That is wonderful when it is written and the ink is drying on the page, but in the beginning it can be scary and frustrating. As any writer knows, the hardest words to write in any new project are the first ones.

Hidden Courage

Such was the case of Princess Jehosheba. She found herself caught in a court drama that would have the wisest, most courageous of us wondering what on earth would happen next. A cameo of Jehosheba is found in 2 Chronicles 22:11–12. You will love this girl when you see what she did. Read the following account, and I will fill in the details later.

> But Jehosheba, King Jehoram's daughter, took Joash, Ahaziah's son. She stole him from among the other sons of the king who were going to be murdered and put him and his nurse in a bedroom. So Jehosheba, who was . . . Ahaziah's sister and the wife of Jehoiada the priest, hid Joash so Athaliah could not kill him. He hid with them in the Temple of God for six years. During that time Athaliah ruled the land.

This is the case of an aunt rescuing her dead brother's son from the evil intentions of his own grandmother, Athaliah. She is what we in the South call "a piece of work." That means she has a lot of complex parts that create a very interesting person. For starters, she is the daughter of Ahab and Jezebel. You do not have to scratch the surface very hard in biblical history to know that this famous duo made our more contemporary Bonnie and Clyde look harmless. They made evil a science.

Athaliah carried on the family tradition of denying God by introducing the worship of Baal to Jehovah's people. She had come from the northern kingdom of Israel to marry Jehoram, the king of Judah (the southern kingdom). She influenced him and her son, Ahaziah, to do "wrong in the eyes of the Lord" (2 Kings 8:18; 2 Chron. 21:4). This woman had no problem with murder, mayhem, or mystery. She was hungry to be in control. When her husband and son died, she was more than ready to step into the position of queen, ruler supreme. There were only a few family members in the way of her unquestioned sovereignty, so she made a plan to have them killed.

This is where our girl, Princess Jehosheba, stepped in and rescued her infant nephew, Joash, the future king. Although he was only a baby, he was in line to be killed with his brothers. Jehosheba could not bear it and secretly got him out of harm's way. She then quietly kept him in the temple of God for six years. All the while, Athaliah was preening her queenly feathers so she could make a good show as the self-appointed queen and card-carrying enemy of God.

Jehosheba saw what she had to do, and she did it. She had no guarantees that her neck would not end up on the chopping block once Athaliah found out about Joash's survival. Like so many people in difficult positions, Jehosheba had to "do what she could and trust God with the rest." That's a safe formula for the person who needs both wisdom and courage. Recognize that humanly you can only do so much, but whatever it is, do it! Also recognize you can trust God to work in ways you cannot know ahead of time. This is called living by faith.

When you are faced with a new story that feels out of control and far beyond anything you ever wanted to write, you need to remember these things:

- *You are not the author of this story.* God is. He knows the end from the beginning. He knows you didn't volunteer to be a character in this story, but for some reason residing deep in the mystery of His heart and brimming with the wonder of His love, you have been chosen to live this story.
- *Don't fall for the line that "God knew He could trust you,"* so that is why you have been cast into an incredible story that requires wisdom and courage to write. That kind of thinking would make anyone shrink from being trustworthy. This is nothing about trusting you. This is about God moving in ways that require you to trust Him. This is not about *your* strength. This is about *His* strength.
- *The wisdom you require will be given. It is not innate.* When you are in the middle of a story that requires wisdom, it has to come from above. It cannot just be what you think is the best thing to do. The book of James addresses this in a few succinct words:

> Who among you is wise and understanding? Let him show
> by his good behavior his deeds in the gentleness of wisdom.
> But if you have bitter jealousy and selfish ambition in your
> heart, do not be arrogant and so lie against the truth. This
> wisdom is not that which comes down from above, but is

earthly, natural, and demonic. For where jealousy and selfish ambition exist, there is disorder and every evil thing. But the wisdom from above is first pure, then peaceable, gentle, reasonable, full of mercy and good fruits, unwavering, without hypocrisy. And the seed whose fruit is righteousness is sown in peace by those who make peace. (3:13–18 NASB)

- *Recognize your need for courage to accompany the wisdom you receive.* You will probably have to do something so unfamiliar to the way you have thought or so difficult that you will not be able to pull it off on your own.

I have a sweet friend who is entering a new phase of her life. She has been propelled into a story she has no taste for writing and no heart for living, but it has been thrust upon her by the increasing dementia of her beloved husband. She is facing the fact that she will have to place him in residential care because he no longer can safely live at home. The *when* and the *where* of her decision will require wisdom. The *how* and the *why* will require courage. She can *know* that she has no choice but to move her husband, whom she loves so much, from their home. She will do it because she has all the wisdom God can give her, but the courage to do it must be given too. The courage must come from God, or she will never be able to make herself do it. Unless God gives her the wisdom and courage combined, she just cannot do it.

- *Remember, you are not going through anything others have not gone through before.* They have found courage and wisdom, and so can you. The scenes may be different, but the basic stories are the same. In a strange sort of way, there is great comfort in this. If others have lived to write new stories, needing courage and wisdom in equal portions, so can you. You can *know*—it will be provided.

No test or temptation that comes your way is beyond the course of what others have had to face. All you need to remember is that God will never let you down; he'll never let you be pushed past your limit; he'll always be there to help you come through it. (1 Cor. 10:13 MSG)

An Overcomer's Courage

Hard things are part of life. If we never face the difficult, we will never have the strength to face what comes next. I am always humbled and inspired by women who have lived lives of courage and wisdom. They survive the unthinkable only to bring greatness to the lives of others. Irene Opdyke was such a woman. In fact, the story of her life was memorialized in the Broadway play *Irina's Vow*. ("Irina" is the Polish spelling of her name.)

Irene was a seventeen-year-old Polish girl who was caught in the misfortunes of history when Russia and Germany invaded Poland. In the chaos that reigned at that time, nine Russian soldiers cornered her and gang-raped her. She ultimately was forced to work in a Russian hospital. When she escaped, she was caught by the Germans and then found herself working in a German munitions factory when Eduard Rueger, a seventy-year-old German major, worked it out for her to be his housekeeper.

A turning point in her story came in 1942. She came upon Jews being sent to their execution. She shuddered as she witnessed a German officer throw a Jewish baby in the air and shoot it. She had to do something, so she began to smuggle food to the Jews in the ghetto. She then moved twelve of the Jews into a space under her employer's gazebo. He never went there, so she thought she could keep them safe.

One day he came home early to find some of the Jews. He was angry but he offered Irene a deal: he would not turn them in to the Gestapo . . . if she would sleep with him. She took the arrangement. She confessed the arrangement to her priest, who told her that her mortal soul was more important than their mortal lives. She made the choice, saying, there were too many lives at stake. So Irene endured his advances, but her Jewish charges remained safe.

One of the Jewish women became pregnant during this time. The word *abortion* came up, but Irene would not hear of it. In 1944, she and the Jews escaped into the Polish forest where the baby boy was born. Shortly after his birth the Russians captured Irene. They planned to send her to Siberia. Through an intervention that could only be called divine, she was maintained in Poland until the end of the war. At that point, her Jewish friends helped her escape to West Germany. There she met her future husband and immigrated to the United States where she started a family and lived quietly. She did not speak of her memories of those years.

Irene's story could have stopped there, but one night a call came to her house that brought her out of her years of silence. A college student was conducting a random survey about whether people believed the Holocaust really happened. That awakened a fiery passion. Irene admitted that by remaining silent through the years, she had allowed evil to win; if we don't speak out, history can repeat itself. So she began giving presentations to schools and service clubs. The little five-foot-tall fireball, who sounded and looked like Zsa Zsa Gabor, began to make waves.

Until her death, Irene spoke out. She was awarded honors and medals while she was alive, as well as after her death, and she has a permanent exhibit in the Holocaust Memorial Museum in Washington, DC; Irene left behind an incredibly well-written story.

There is a little postscript to this story. It made me smile after all the trauma of Irene's story. After the war, Major Rueger returned to Germany. His wife shunned him because of his keeping eighteen-year-old Irene as a mistress, and he ended up living on the streets. The Jewish couple who was among those hidden under his gazebo took him in. And their son, the baby born in the forest, grew up and one day came to New York to attend the play that was the story of his beloved benefactor.

> Irene admitted that by remaining silent through the years, she had allowed evil to win.

Irene's daughter told the story of how positive her mother became through forgiveness, telling everyone she met that one person can make a difference. She was a very positive person. Her mother was not bitter, and she said if she had to do it again, she would. As long as there is life, there's hope.[1]

Facing the Evil Queen

I love Irene's story. And like Irene, Princess Jehosheba had to decide what she would do in the face of unrestrained evil. Let's take a look at evil Queen Athaliah's backstory:

The people of Jerusalem chose Ahaziah, Jehoram's youngest son, to be king in his place. The robbers who had come with the Arabs to attack Jehoram's camp had killed all of Jehoram's older sons. So Ahaziah began to rule Judah. Ahaziah was twenty-two years old when he became king, and he ruled one year in Jerusalem. His mother's name was Athaliah, a grand-daughter of Omri. Ahaziah followed the ways of Ahab's family, because his mother encouraged him to do wrong. Ahaziah did what the LORD said was wrong, as Ahab's family had done. They gave advice to Ahaziah after his father died, and their bad advice led to his death. (2 Chron. 22:1–4)

His death then sent his mother on a murderous rampage. She was not in *grief*; she was in *greed*. She wanted what she wanted and there was nothing she would not do to get it.

"When Ahaziah's mother, Athaliah, saw that her son was dead, she killed all the royal family in Judah" (22:10) . . . except one. What a family dynamic! Can you imagine the tension and angst that went on during those years? Few of us have to live despairing for our physical lives, fearing that our own families will kill us. Jehosheba knew she was in a dangerous situation but she survived! She survived physically, saved her nephew physically, and kept her senses throughout the whole ordeal.

Then came the day when Joash would be presented as the real king in Athalia's usurped kingdom. It was a great day and an infamous day. No one would have trouble remembering where he or she was the day Joash was declared king! Read the account and try to see the colors and smell the smells of that unforgetta-ble day. You might imagine yourself as Jehosheba, standing to the side, watching it all in wonder. Her husband, the priest Jehoiada, had decided to do something! The story is told in 2 Chronicles 23:3, 6–16:

> Jehoiada said to them, "The king's son will rule, as the Lord promised about David's descendants . . . Don't let anyone come into the Temple of the LORD except the priests and Levites who serve . . . The Levites must stay near the king, each man with his weapon in his hand. If anyone tries to enter the Temple, kill him. Stay close to the king when he goes in and when he goes out." Then Jehoiada told the soldiers where to stand with weapon in hand. There were guards from the south side of the Temple to the north side. They stood by the altar and the Temple and around the king. Jehoiada and his sons brought out the king's son and put the crown on him and gave him a copy of the agreement. Then they appointed him king and poured olive oil on him and shouted, "Long live the king!"
>
> When Athaliah heard the noise of the people running and praising the king, she went to them at the Temple of the LORD. She looked, and there was the king standing by his pillar at the entrance. The officers and the trumpeters were standing beside him, and all the people of the land were happy and blowing trumpets. The singers were playing musical instruments and leading praises. Then Athaliah tore her clothes and screamed, "Traitors! Traitors!"
>
> Jehoiada the priest sent out the commanders of a hundred men, who led the army. He said, "Surround her with soldiers and take her out of the Temple area. Kill with a sword anyone who follows her." He had said, "Don't put Athaliah to death in the Temple of the LORD." So they caught her when she came to

the entrance of the Horse Gate near the palace. There they put her to death. Then Jehoiada made an agreement with the people and the king that they would be the LORD's special people.

Ripples in the Water

It is one thing to take action when you have no other choice. It is another thing entirely when you can choose safety instead. Jehosheba could have chosen to shrink into the background, play it safe, and let Athaliah murder her little nephew, Joash. Instead, she took a huge personal risk. With extraordinary courage and wisdom, she acted to save the boy and keep him hidden for six long years until the time was right for her husband to step out in opposition to the usurping queen.

As a result of Jehosheba's wisdom and the courage to use it, Joash was protected, and at age seven he became king of Judah. He ruled Israel for more than forty years, rebuilt the temple of God, and saved Jerusalem from being captured. How did he manage all of that? It is because, as 2 Kings 12:2 says, "Joash did what the LORD said was right."

Imagine the impact Jehosheba's unselfish actions had over those forty years! Like the ripples that go out when a stone is cast into a lake, we never know how far our influence extends. Our job is just to drop the stone in the water. God will magnify and use our small actions to His own glory, and the ripples will continue, perhaps forever.

Personal Reflection

1. Esther is considered one of the great female heroes in the Bible. Do you think you are anything like Esther? Explain how that makes you feel.
2. What trait of Esther's do you most wish you possessed? Why?
3. Is there a situation in your life today where you know what to do, but you lack the courage to do it? Describe.
4. Jehosheba put herself at great risk in order to protect her tiny nephew, Joash. Do you think you would do that for a baby in your family? Explain.
5. If you could write a new story and become more like Jehosheba, how do you see yourself changing your life?
6. What spiritual lesson can you apply to your life this week from the life of Jehosheba? Explain.
7. If you took the risk to start a new, more courageous story, who else do you think would be affected?

Journal Entry

To continue your new story, complete the following starter sentence in your personal journal. Then continue writing thoughts and feelings from your heart as long as you need to.

The action I most need to take in my life that will require wisdom and courage is . . .

Group Discussion Questions

1. In this chapter, what did we learn about Athaliah?

2. How did Athaliah counsel her son, the king, Ahaziah?

3. What did Jehu, who would become the next king of Israel in the North, do to Ahaziah?

4. How did Athaliah take advantage of the situation?

5. Who was Jehosheba? How was she related to King Ahaziah? And, therefore, how was she related to Joash?

6. What wise and courageous action did she take?

7. Would Joash's life have been in danger had Jehosheba not acted? Why?

8. What risk did Jehosheba take in saving the young prince? Explain your reasoning.

9. Where, and for how long, did she hide the boy?

10. What spiritual lessons can we draw from the life of Jehosheba?

11. Why do you think Joash was blessed by God to reign for forty years?

Chapter 8

GET PAST
THE RESISTANCE
OF FEAR

Many of our fears are tissue-paper-thin, and a single courageous step would carry us clear through them.

—Brendan Francis

Abigail

Abigail was caught between two powerful
men, but she did not buckle under fear.

1 SAMUEL 25:2–42

Abigail's husband, Nabal, was by definition a "fool." And his
actions bore that out in giant letters.

Think about it: David, king of Israel, and his soldiers went to
the trouble to protect Nabal's shepherds from their enemy neighbors. Then David did what was customary for such "protection."
He sent some of his men to ask Nabal for some food and provisions. Instead, Nabal insulted David! Now *that* was the behavior
of a foolish man. You just do not insult the king and live to tell
about it!

King David gathered up four hundred of his soldiers and
headed over to kill Nabal and everybody in his family. Nabal, of
course, had no clue what was happening. He was too busy being
foolish. But his wise wife, Abigail, found out and decided to do
something to protect her family. Piling food and provisions on
donkeys, she set out to face the angry king.

Abigail was probably terrified, but she "did it scared." What
happened next was all part of God's script for her. She played the
role; He directed the play.

Charlene was a tremendously gifted woman. She wrote poetry and painted and dreamed that someday she would write a novel. She talked about writing a novel, told her friends she wanted to write a novel, and approached every author she knew, saying, "I want to write a novel." She talked a lot about a novel.

Megan was married to a man who raged at her and at their children. He pushed her from time to time and generally kept her walking on eggshells. Megan talked about doing something about her marital disaster, she told her friends she wanted to do something about her marital disaster, and she approached every pastor she knew, saying, "I want to do something about my marital disaster." She talked a lot about her marital disaster.

Whether you are soaring on a new dream or climbing out of a miry pit, you must take responsibility and act.

Charlene never wrote her fantasized novel, and Megan did nothing about her shabby marriage. They both were stuck. They both thought they wanted to go forward. They both knew how to talk about their plans. Neither, however, had gotten past the unseen resistance that was holding them back from moving forward.

Talking a good game is one of the major blocks to writing a new story. It is always easier to *talk about* writing a new story than actually putting pen to paper and doing it. This is true for writers as well as life-livers. New stories mean change; new experiences, new situations, new people, hard work, and honestly—it usually just feels easier to stay put. I have often heard it said, "Better the devil you know than the devil you don't."[1] Of course, dealing with the devil is never easy, but something about the familiar draws us and many times holds us. It is comfortable. It is non-threatening. It is home.

In contrast, something about the unfamiliar feels frightening. Questions arise in our minds, such as, what am I going to do, how am I going to do it, and is this really the right thing to do? These questions permeate our decisions about writing new stories. Whether you are soaring on a new dream or climbing out of a miry pit, you must take responsibility and act. You are the one responsible to make a move, and you are the one who must take action. No one but you can propel your story forward. Oh sure, people along the way may give you a kick where it counts and inspire you along the way, but you are the one to say, "This is it. I'm staying in this pit." As one lady said, "I've come to like my pit. It's comfortable. It's me. I think I'll just carpet it and air condition it and stay."

You are also the one to say, "This is *not* it. I will follow my dream instead." The cool factor for the Christian is that you do not have to make this move alone. God never wants to leave you in that pit. He never desires for your story to end there. He is a redeemer of our messes, and He takes great pleasure in even our feeble steps toward healthy, new, life-giving stories.

Cousins

I met Christa at a women's conference several years ago. She had some responsibility that had us working closely together. She is a young, single African-American woman, and I am an older, married, Anglo-American woman. Somehow, during the course of our interaction, we dubbed one another "Cousin." Christa has stayed in touch with me over the years, and I have seen her write an amazing new story in her life.

When we first met, Christa was the typical young Christian woman, trying to find her place in God's plan. Her conversations with me via e-mail were scattered and few. I had no idea what God had planned for her, but I knew she would keep me informed.

Her story started to take on new proportions when two young girls came into her life. They lived in the same apartment building with her, so she knew their comings and goings pretty well. They were young, neglected, and pretty much on their own. That would not do as far as Cousin was concerned. She began to offer shelter to the girls and to take an interest in their lives. I began to receive little notes about her concern for them and her interactions with their mother and dealings with the court.

Christa moved from being a woman in search of a place to belong into the role of mother of two girls who are now eleven and fifteen. She has cared for them, seen that they were well schooled, introduced them to the Christian faith, and given them a place of sanctuary. She has made a home for them, and in the process, she has found her true strength—mothering children! She is now working toward becoming the owner and director of a first-class daycare center.

I am thrilled for Cousin. She is writing a new story, and in the process she has rescued two young girls from a pit that could have been their ruination. It has not been an easy process. She could have chosen just to mind her own business, not to get involved, and to run after her own self-fulfillment. She chose another road—as Robert Frost described it, "The Road Less Traveled." Without any idea of what would happen, she gave two girls a way to write new stories in their lives while she wrote a new story in hers.

God Is Greater

God also is the giver of our dreams. Philippians 2:12–13 says, "Keep on working to complete your salvation with fear and trembling, because God is working in you to help you want to do and be able to do what pleases him." I believe with everything in me that God gives us our *want-to* and our *how-to* for bringing about His delight. The problem lies with us when we know and believe He has something for us to do, but we balk because it is scary or unfamiliar.

Linda Strom is a woman who has written a unique story with her life as she has followed the want-to and the how-to God put in her.

Linda grew up in Pennsylvania, the daughter of a physically abusive, alcoholic dad and a verbally abusive mother. Her grandmother, who loved her unconditionally and prayed for her regularly, gave her hope as she often told Linda, "God is always greater!"

Linda wrote on her Web site, "In April of 1963, I married

Dallas Strom. I brought some ingredients into my marriage that had been modeled to me in my home. Dallas was a tease and seemed to enjoy watching me lose control. One day in anger, I threw a pot of hot baked beans at Dallas and hit him. He walked out the door, and I was alone and desperate. As I was on my knees cleaning up the beans, I cried out, 'God, if You're real, You've got to help me because if You're not, I'm not going to make it in this world.'"

Linda's story had come to a halt. All of her fears had met at an intersection in her mind. If she was going to write a new story, God would have to do it for her. Her old story was just too overwhelming for her to change it by herself.

The night she threw the beans was a real change point for Linda. Billy Graham was on TV speaking about, of all things, marriage. Linda said,

> How I wanted to change! But Dr. Graham said that in ourselves we don't have the power to change. Then he read, "But as many as received him, to them gave he power to become the sons of God, even to them that believe on his name" (John 1:12 KJV). I wondered, *Does Jesus really have the power to make me different?*
>
> Dr. Graham talked about God's love for me. I had longed for love, but I had lost my heart out of fear. That night I confessed my sins and my need for God. A deep sense of being loved and belonging settled into my soul. When Dallas returned home, I eagerly told him of my experience. I'll never forget his response: "It should be a lot safer around here if what you say is true!" And indeed it was.

Later that year, Dallas attended a Billy Graham crusade in Nebraska. In the car on the way home, he invited Jesus into his heart. Linda said, "My grandma's words rang true in my heart: 'God is always greater.'"

Linda's life today is nothing that she expected. Her beloved Dallas has gone home now. Linda is still here ministering in prisons all over the world. She is living a story that could have ended with a pot of beans being used as a weapon, but "God was greater."

Facing Your Fear

Fear will do a number on you when you begin to dream a new dream and move in a new direction. It will keep you making excuses for not getting started and rationalizing why you are making no progress. People around you may not understand. They will ask such questions as, why do you want to do something new? Isn't where you are now *good enough*? My question is, good enough for what? Settling for the status quo will keep you living in the familiar, but you will never have the adventure of what lies just beyond what you know.

Fear has an odd way of disguising itself, and it affects us in different ways. Fear grabs you at your most vulnerable place. For instance, fear of criticism is a big one for many people. Being misunderstood and rejected for choices you are making can be hard, but you must address it.

Kelly found that out when she was left as a widow with three little children. She parented them alone for three years until she met Bob at a church function. They became friendly, and a year later, they married. All was well for a few months, and then Bob began to display some disturbing behaviors that took Kelly and the children totally by surprise. His seemingly mild manner became morose and dark. He spent as much time as possible alone. He had little to say to the children or to Kelly. None of them understood. Bob rejected Kelly's pleas for him to see a physician, a pastor, or anyone to help him. He just became more and more inward and coldly angry.

One night Kelly woke up to Bob pressing his pillow over her head. She told him to stop, but he kept on until she rolled out of her side of the bed. She went to the living room and lay on the couch, terrified and waiting for morning. What was going on? Was Bob trying to kill her? How much longer was she going to live in this insanity and subject her children to Bob's irrational behavior? When morning came, there was no explanation. A sullen Bob left the house for work.

Kelly decided it was time to do something. When she called her pastor, he was appropriately sympathetic but reminded her that she would have to speak to a committee of men, who would need some explanations as to why she needed to do something. Kelly agreed to meet with them and told them what had been happening, including the pillow incident. One of the older men upbraided her and commented, "Bob didn't commit adultery, so I don't know why you are here." The criticism played into her fear. She left the meeting totally upset with herself. Had she done the wrong thing by going to the church? Eventually she got a grip and began to speak truth to her fear: *That was one man's opinion. He never has walked in my shoes. I can't continue to live like this and I won't.*

Kelly began to move forward in a slow and arduous journey, but today Kelly is a mature, bright, single mom again. She has discovered that she can live a new way without the approval of everyone else in her life. Her children are becoming delightful young people, and their home is free of the chaos of not knowing what will happen next.

Abigail

One of my favorite women in the Scriptures is Abigail. Look how she is described and what her situation in life was. (Trust me, you will find someone to admire in Abigail. We would say in Tennessee, "She doesn't mess around!")

> A man in Maon who had land at Carmel was very rich. He had three thousand sheep and a thousand goats. He was cutting the wool off his sheep at Carmel. His name was Nabal, and he was a descendant of Caleb. His wife was named Abigail. She was wise and beautiful, but Nabal was cruel and mean. (1 Sam. 25:2–3)

Right there we have the potential for a lot of fear and anguish. Anytime you have to deal with someone who is cruel and mean, you have trouble. Nabal was a man marked by a name as a child: Fool. Who knows if he lived up to his name, or if his mother just knew in her heart that she had borne a fool? Either way, as an adult, Abigail is the one who had to deal with him.

Imagine some of the scenarios Abigail might have faced in her life with Nabal. She was a woman of wisdom, which is the grace of having an intelligent attitude toward life. Having to live under the shadow of Nabal had probably taught her a lot about how to be wise in handling troublesome situations he had instigated.

I have a friend who came from a family where the beauty and intelligence of her mother saved her and her siblings from the outrageous harangues of her father. It was not a happy family. Everyone lived on eggshells, but they were saved from what might have been far worse because their mother ran interference and protected them from his angry outbursts. Unfortunately, that family never looked for a new story. They believed they were captives of their father's absurdities and saw no way to escape.

Their father eventually died. That is how his wife and children escaped. The tragedy of the whole story was that by the time he died, no one had the heart left to do differently. They had become like circus elephants trained as babies to stand in place by having huge chains hooked around their ankles connected to a thick stake in the ground. When the chains were removed, all that was needed to control them was a thin piece of twine that one yank of their mammoth foot could easily have broken. They never tried, though, because they no longer believed they could. No new story for them. They were bound by their own minds.

She was a woman of wisdom, which is the grace of having an intelligent attitude toward life.

Many times I have seen women settle for the status quo due to fear of what *might* happen and fear of having no place to go. This especially happens when a woman is in a relationship with a fool. In my years of work as a counselor and recently in my work as a life coach, I have encountered women who are fearful of even thinking about a different life because they have allowed a fool to chain their emotions to an invisible stake.

A fool, by the way, always thinks he is right. "The way of a fool is right in his own eyes, but a wise man is he who listens to counsel" (Prov. 12:15 NASB). He uses anger to control. "When a wise man has a controversy with a foolish man, the foolish man either rages or laughs" (Prov. 29:9 NASB). And he trusts in his own heart: "The fool has said in his heart, 'There is no God'" (Ps. 14:1 NASB).[2]

What If I Were Not Scared?

A good question to ask yourself when you want to write a new story but are fearful is this: what could I do if I were not scared?

Sharon was raised in a home where her mother was determined that her only daughter was going to be a hypochondriac ruled by fear. The mother was focused on being sick, so she convinced her daughter to be sick as well. She did everything she could to keep her daughter in a cocoon of disease. Actually, she did everything she could to make her believe that she had to take extraordinary measures to save herself from whatever might be in the air. When Sharon condescended to wearing a mask everywhere she went, because her mother had convinced her that pollen would clog her lungs and prohibit her breathing, she woke up one day and came to her senses. She realized that her mother's fears had overtaken her and that she was living in the tale of fear her mother was writing for her. She answered the question, what would I do if I weren't scared? with, "I would do a lot!" And then she did.

Sharon began to venture into areas her mother had told her would make her sick or would exacerbate her allergies. Amazingly, she found she could survive and even do well. She went so far as to travel abroad several times and to take a job that she loved—in a germ factory known as an elementary school! When she shook off her old fears, she found a new direction. She had bought into some childhood *stuff* that carried over for a long time. She was the only one who could stand up to her fear with boldness and move in the right direction.

Have you ever heard yourself whine? It is such an unattractive thing to do. When you are talking a good game about why you cannot write a new story, many times you will hear yourself listing all the reasons why you are stuck. Fear is definitely one of them, but sometimes you will even hear yourself complaining that you cannot move on because you are too old or maybe too young. Then there is the *woman* thing. It goes, "I am a woman, and the glass ceiling always stops me." Maybe you complain that your look is too youthful to be taken seriously (yes, I've heard that), or maybe you complain because your skin is too dark, your hair is too thin, your nose is too long, or your teeth are too crooked. The truth is, if you want a reason to stay where you are, you can find it. It is there, right in front of you. Comfort zones are easy to hang on to, but they usually are more about what we are afraid of than what we love.

Quirky Fears

It is not uncommon to have quirky little thoughts that rise up and cause you to bolt at the suggestion of changes in your life. Those fears often have to do with perceptions that gnaw at you like squirrels gnawing on an ear of corn. You start out with great confidence that you should and can be moving forward, but then little pieces of your strength and confidence go missing, and you are left with a good idea but no way to make it happen.

One of my sweet friends is called to minister to people who have no money. No matter what she does for them, they cannot pay for it or even give her a donation. She has to supply all of the funds, but she has a quirky little fear. She has a hard time bringing herself to believe that it is okay to sell the beautiful note cards she makes in churches where she speaks about her ministry. She can receive an offering, but selling what she makes feels really *out there* to her. I felt compelled to ask her, "Where is that written? Where did you get the idea that it was not okay to sell something in a church in order to support your ministry?"

It occurred to her that a long time ago she had heard disparaging remarks from people in her church about someone selling cookies in the lobby. She did not know why the person was selling the cookies, but it put a sour taste in her mouth for any kind of selling even if it was to support a ministry. My friend was faced with one of those quirky fears that had no basis in fact but really tormented and held her back. She wanted to minister with passion and help support her ministry through the cards she made, but the truth was she could not sell them if she did not make them available. And yet she was afraid of being considered materialistic.

Like many of us, my friend had to come to grips with her own personal quirky fear. When we are faced with those, we either have to quit what we are doing because it is clearly wrong or get over it. Quirky fears will not leave you alone until you dig deep enough to know what is blocking you, or you discover there is no block, so you just get over it!

You might have discovered one of your quirky fears. We all have them. You may not call it a fear, but it is a thinking pattern that stands in the way of your going forward with a new story. It usually comes from something we have said to ourselves, usually in the form of a vow, or something said by a significant person in our lives.

I had a wonderful English teacher when I was growing up. She was a recent college graduate and close to the age of the senior high kids she taught, although she was "Miss Roberts" to me. Even though I was a teenager during those years, I could see she was held back by fear. I could not identify it as a quirky fear then, but looking back, I see it. She told me her minister father had blocked her marriage to her high school sweetheart, Thad, because her dad said he would not stay around for the long haul.

The very sad Miss Roberts obeyed her father and did not marry Thad, but she moved a thousand miles from home to be a teacher in a different city. She found great acceptance among her students and other faculty members. She was warm, gregarious, and a great teacher, but the thought of moving on emotionally and living a new life without her Thad was just beyond her.

If she were to find a new relationship, it would mean leaving behind the old story of thwarted love. She could not let someone new come into her life because she would be closing the book on her long-gone boyfriend. Of course, Thad had moved on in his life, but Miss Roberts could not face that reality. That would be proving her father right. She made some vows when it all fell apart: "I will love him forever (whether he stays around or not), and my father will not be right about Thad."

Miss Roberts spent a lot of time reading the poems of Edna St. Vincent Millay, a wonderful poet, but a woman given to clinging to old stories as the last verse of her "Ashes of Life" reflects:

> *Love has gone and left me, and the neighbors knock and borrow,*
> *And life goes on forever like the gnawing of a mouse.*
> *And to-morrow and to-morrow and to-morrow and to-morrow*
> *There's this little street and this little house.*[3]

Miss Roberts was stuck, and her story ended in her vow. She had a quirky fear based in her past experience and the vows she made. She would not love again, and from everything I could see, she would not live again. She was determined to drag her old feelings forward, not realizing or wanting to admit that there might be fresh, new life out there just beyond the horizon, if she would quit clinging to her quirky fears and connections to the past. It was time to get over it and move on.

Getting Unstuck from Our Fears

God is such a faithful storyteller in our lives. He never desires to leave us stuck where we are. If we find ourselves there, it is because we have made the choice to stay while telling ourselves this is all we can do, or this is all we were meant for, or maybe life is over so I will hang out here until I die. That usually is unspoken, but it rides on the surface of our thinking, affecting everything we think, hope, or dream. It causes us to resist the possibilities and to remain stuck.

I was talking to a life coach friend of mine about the resistance we often encounter that keeps us stuck. Here's what she said:

I know. I've been there. Sometimes we can even get stuck in the goodness we have going for us too. About ten years ago, I began to believe God wanted me to change my counseling focus. I had worked for almost twenty years as a social worker, providing counseling for individuals and families. I loved the work, but it required that I be on call every other weekend, as well as weeknights. I had recently had some books published and had begun traveling some. I badly needed a change of pace, as well as more flexibility in my days.

As I continued to pray, I just *happened* to be introduced to the first life coach I had ever met. The responsibilities of life coaching sounded like a perfect fit to me. However, my husband made several good points about why I should not give up the good opportunity I had enjoyed for years. He pointed out that life coaching was a new frontier, and nobody knew exactly what it was. Of course, he also addressed the degree of financial security I enjoyed. He reminded me of the ways God had used me in my counseling position, repeating various reports that he had received over the years from people who had been my clients. He reminded me of the fruit of my gifting. I listened, but the voice of the Holy Spirit still spoke "change" to me.

Finally, I told my husband that, even though I agreed with the points he had made, I needed to obey God and make the change. He decided to support me in that decision.

In order to carry out my plan, I had to find someone to lease my half of the counseling office for six months. I had decided I wanted to create a home office and reduce my expenses, to be more casual in my attire and less scheduled.

Several days after I made my decision, a recent graduate from the school of social work called to ask about work opportunities. I told him about my half of the office space my associate and I were renting being available. He was thrilled! Within a week he had met with my associate, and they reached an agreement on all arrangements. Because I left him the furnishings I owned in the office, all he had to do was walk in with a file cabinet! He was happy, and so was I.

By the time I followed each step of obedience, I had no leading to continue to maintain my social work license. I did not renew it that year. I burned that bridge so that, if I encountered difficulties in my new venture, I would not be tempted to turn back. In my heart, I felt that my work as a social worker was finished. I began enjoying success in life coaching. God supplied me with wonderful clients, who truly seek to get unstuck and find their next step in life, a life coach's dream!

From that experience, I learned that sometimes success can become a trap too. We can be afraid to let go of the *goodness* we have been given in the past to take hold of God's future provisions.

It is hard to leave a sure thing for an unsure thing. It is a challenge to our stability and all that we find comfortable. Yet sometimes God has better plans for the one who will let go of the comfortable to pursue the not so comfortable. Sometimes it's all there is to do.

Face-to-Face with Fear

Let's go back to our brave sister, Abigail. You have already seen that she was wise and beautiful, and her husband was mean and cruel. There is definitely a story brewing! King David came to the desert of Maon where Nabal lived. David was accompanied by four hundred of his men, who had to eat and find water. They came upon Nabal's men, shearing sheep. David's men did what was customary at that time—they offered the sheep herders a little protection, and in return for their services, food and water were expected. So David sent ten men to Nabal to request the supplies.

If you understand the culture of that day, it made a lot of sense. Anyone who did business in the desert had to be alert to marauding bands of Arabs, who preyed on whoever they could find. David and his band of men had acted graciously toward Nabal. Their presence was a buffer to keep bandits from bothering Nabal's men while they sheared the sheep. If for no other reason, Nabel should have offered his protectors the all-important hospitality of the Middle East.

> When David's men arrived, they gave the message to Nabal, but Nabal insulted them. He answered them, "Who is David? Who is this son of Jesse? Many slaves are running away from their masters today! I have bread and water, and I have meat that I killed for my servants who cut the wool. But I won't give it to men I don't know." (1 Sam. 25:9–11)

If you had to come up with a list of words to describe Nabal and his behavior, what would they be? We already have *mean* and *cruel* from our first introduction to Nabal. How many more words could you add to that list? *Selfish? Inhospitable?* Just plain *foolish?* Those words describe Abigail's husband. Then "David's men went back and told him all Nabal had said. Then David said to them, 'Put on your swords!' So they put on their swords, and David put on his also. About four hundred men went with David, but two hundred men stayed with the supplies" (vv. 12–13).

Uh-oh. David is the king, and he has been insulted. He has four hundred men with swords ready to go into action. He was not just putting them through practice maneuvers either because he strapped a sword on himself as well. He meant business.

> One of Nabal's servants said to Abigail, Nabal's wife, "David sent messengers from the desert to greet our master, but Nabal insulted them. These men were very good to us. They did not harm us. They stole nothing from us during all the time we were out in the field with them. Night and day they protected us. They were like a wall around us while we were with them caring for the sheep. Now think about it, and decide what you can do. Terrible trouble is coming to our master and all his family. Nabal is such a wicked man that no one can even talk to him." (vv. 14–17)

If you had been told that "terrible trouble" was coming to you and your family, what would be your first thought? *Run! Hide! Pray!* It was clear that Nabal would be no help, so Abigail had to do something quickly to protect her family, in spite of her foolish husband.

> Abigail hurried. She took two hundred loaves of bread, two leather bags full of wine, five cooked sheep, a bushel of cooked grain, a hundred cakes of raisins, and two hundred cakes of pressed figs and put all these on donkeys. Then she told her

servants, "Go on. I'll follow you." But she did not tell her husband. (vv. 18–19)

Well, duh! Why *would* she tell him? He might just do something else foolish and get them into even more trouble with King David. Abigail was obviously wiser than Nabal, so she went out to meet trouble face-to-face: "Abigail rode her donkey and came down toward the mountain hideout. There she met David and his men coming down toward her" (v. 20). Can you imagine the terror Abigail likely felt at that moment? What would David do to her out of his frustration and anger toward Nabal? Kill her? And a bigger question for this worried woman: should she fear King David or wicked Nabal the most? If Abigail did not feel any fear, she was one amazing woman. Her husband was a fool, who was cruel, mean, and had ticked off the king. Someone was going to die if Abigail did not do something, so she did the wise thing—she faced it! She summoned her courage and went toward trouble, instead of running from it.

David had just said, "It's been useless! I watched over Nabal's property in the desert. I made sure none of his sheep was missing. I did good to him, but he has paid me back with evil. May God punish my enemies even more. I will not leave one of Nabal's men alive until morning."

When Abigail saw David, she quickly got off her donkey and bowed facedown on the ground before him. She fell at David's feet and said, "My master, let the blame be on me! Please let me talk to you. Listen to what I say. My master, don't pay attention to this worthless man Nabal. He is like his name. His name means 'fool,' and he is truly a fool. But I, your servant, didn't see the men you sent." (vv. 21–25)

If you are going to write a new story, facing reality is part of the first step. Why do you think Abigail thought it necessary to explain that Nabal was a fool? (As if King David had not already figured that one out himself!) Watch how she explains things to David by taking the blame and giving him a blessing to encourage his heart:

> The LORD will certainly let your family have many kings, because you fight his battles. As long as you live, may you do nothing bad. Someone might chase you to kill you, but the LORD your God will keep you alive. He will throw away your enemies' lives as he would throw a stone from a sling. The LORD will keep all his promises of good things for you. He will make you leader over Israel. Then you won't feel guilty or troubled because you killed innocent people and punished them. Please remember me when the LORD brings you success. (vv. 28–31)

Those are the words of a wise woman—a woman who faced her fear in order to begin a new relationship with King David. And it worked! Notice how her bravery and humble wisdom affected David:

> David answered Abigail, "Praise the LORD, the God of Israel, who sent you to meet me. May you be blessed for your wisdom. You have kept me from killing or punishing people today. As surely as the LORD, the God of Israel, lives,

he has kept me from hurting you. If you hadn't come quickly to meet me, not one of Nabal's men would have lived until morning."

Then David accepted Abigail's gifts. He told her, "Go home in peace. I have heard your words, and I will do what you have asked." (vv. 32–35)

And those are the words of a wise *man*! When he heard Abigail's reasoning and wisdom, based on her belief in God, he recognized their truth and made a godly decision in response. She was brilliant! And facing her fear allowed Abigail to save her entire family, including her cruel husband who got them into the mess in the first place. Ironic, isn't it?

That sounds like a great place for this story to end, right? But no! There is more. Abigail went home and found Nabal in the house eating and drinking "like a king." In fact, he was drunk and in an uncharacteristically good mood. Abigail let him have his food and drink and did not tell him anything until the next day, when she told him everything that had happened while he was making merry. Clearly, that was too much information for him because his heart stopped, and he went rigid. Ten days later, "the Lord struck Nabal and he died" (v. 38).

When David heard that Nabal was dead, he said, "Praise the Lord! Nabal insulted me, but the Lord has supported me! He has kept me from doing wrong. The Lord has punished Nabal for his wrong" (v. 39).

Then David wasted no time sending his servants to ask Abigail if she would be his wife. "Abigail bowed facedown on the ground and said, 'I am your servant. I'm ready to serve you and to wash the feet of my master's servants.' Abigail quickly got on a donkey and went with David's messengers, with her five maids following her. And she became David's wife" (vv. 41–42).

From Victim to Victory

Wow! From the wife of a cruel, mean, foolish drunkard to the wife of one of Israel's wisest and most godly kings! Abigail went from abused and tormented woman to queen of the land in short order because she resisted her fear and moved forward with determination. Then David and Abigail wasted no time writing a new story together, which was obviously God's plan.

Sometimes the first chapter of a new story is also the last chapter of an old story. They overlap, and the change from old to new is seamless when we allow God to write the transition sentence.

Personal Reflection

1. Have you ever found yourself in a story similar to Abigail's old story? Describe.
2. How does it make you feel when someone abuses you or treats you badly?
3. What is the biggest fear in your life that you are allowing to hold you back from writing a new story?
4. How do you think you can begin to move forward? Explain.
5. What do you most wish you could emulate about Abigail? Why?
6. Name two things you can do this week to begin overcoming your fear of writing a new story. Be specific.
7. How does God fit into your plan to move forward?
8. What transition sentence do you hear God writing between your old story and your new one?

Journal Entry

To continue your new story, complete the following starter sentence in your personal journal. Then continue writing thoughts and feelings from your heart as long as you need to.

I know I need to overcome my fear of _____ by taking these first steps forward in my life . . .

Group Discussion Questions

1. Looking back (the gift of hindsight), what do you think were the major turning points in Abigail's story?
2. Name one fear that might have overcome her, if she had let it.
3. A dear older woman gave some good advice that I think we all could heed. It makes the new stories easier to come by. She says, "Face it. Just face it." How well do you think Abigail faced her situation?
4. Do you think Abigail had plans prior to this situation to write a new story? Why?
5. What was Abigail's appeal to David?
6. Why do you think she said so much to David about the Lord?
7. What did David recognize in Abigail?
8. Who did he credit with keeping him out of trouble?
9. What strikes you about Nabal's lack of concern for what was going on with his wife?
10. Why do you think Abigail waited until Nabal was sober to tell him how she had thwarted King David's attack against him and his house? Wouldn't he have taken it better if he'd been a little drunk?
11. How was God involved in creating Abigail's new story?
12. Maybe you can identify some of your fears, based on this list from Gallup Polls in 2001 that shows what percentage of people suffer from fear of each item. Do you see yourself in this list? If so, where?

- Snakes: 51 percent
- Speaking in public: 40 percent
- Heights: 36 percent
- Being closed in a small space: 34 percent
- Spiders and insects: 27 percent
- Needles and getting shots: 21 percent
- Mice: 20 percent
- Flying on a plane: 18 percent
- Dogs (sorry, Lassie): 11 percent
- Thunder and lightning: 11 percent
- Crowds: 11 percent
- Going to the doctor: 9 percent

13. What is necessary in order to move forward when fear is blocking your way?

Chapter 9

CHOOSE
TO BOUNCE
BACK

What the caterpillar calls the end of the world the master calls a butterfly.

—Richard Bach

Naaman's Servant Girl

Naaman's servant girl was kidnapped and
held captive, but she lived a life of
resilient integrity.

2 KINGS 5:1–4

She was an ordinary little girl, living at home, doing all the normal things little girls do. Suddenly, the army of Aram attacked her town, and she was stolen from her family and home. Under the command of a man named Naaman, she was taken to a foreign country and made to serve Naaman's wife.

Naaman, the girl's new master, had a skin disease, which evidently caused him to suffer. He was a man, and she was a little girl. She did not know if his problem was as passing as poison ivy or as permanent as leprosy. But if you had been the servant girl in captivity, would you have felt sorry for him? Would you have wanted to help him? Or would you have wished the disease would worsen and, perhaps, even take his life?

This little servant girl had some difficult choices to make. She could stay focused on her old story of captivity and anger, or she could exercise the *instead* option and refocus on the future and a new story. The choice she made and its effect on Naaman will surely surprise you!

Amy Carmichael, missionary to India, has been a mentor to me for more than thirty years. The fact that she died in 1951 when I was a very young girl has made very little difference. Whenever I pick up one of her books, I read for a few minutes, and God always seems to be waiting in the shadows, encouraging me to "get this" or "remember that." She was a picture of resilience, and she has impacted lives of people all over the world. She was a woman who gave her life to save children who were sold into Hindu temple prostitution in India. She loved her work and knew God had called her to it, but then her circumstances changed dramatically.

One dark night Amy fell into a pit that was dug inside an old house where she and her students were taking shelter. Her body was jolted, broken, and irreparably damaged. She was taken to her home in the missionary compound to recuperate. In those days there was no such thing as physical therapy. She was put to bed and attended to in every loving way her coworkers and students could offer, but it was evident she would never again be able to do the things she had always done. Her active days were over. She could either fold up her tent and call it quits or choose to bounce back and do whatever she could within her limitations. Amy Carmichael chose to bounce back. She did not get better physically; in fact, much of the remainder of her life was spent in pain. She did, however, keep going, reaching out and touching the lives of other people.

Amy began to write. She wrote prolifically and with great intimacy. She could no longer go out to remote villages to save the children, but she could write words of encouragement and hope to those who could go. She connected with people all over the world who at one time had been part of the Dohnavur Fellowship, the home for the abused children that she and her compatriots had founded many years before. She also connected with me. Through her writings, I saw the soul of a magnificent woman who knew she was on this earth for a purpose, and until God called her home, she had every intention of living life to the max.

I was deeply encouraged by her words when I was going through a particularly difficult struggle years ago. She had written a letter specifically for her student, but someone had had the forethought to save her writings. Then, so many years later, I read the letter, and the words were tailor-made for me. Maybe they will be for you too:

> You are now in a good position to prove that gift of joy. It is easy to rejoice when everything is as one wishes it were. But when things are exactly as one wishes they were *not*, it is not so easy. *Then* is the time to prove the things we believe. Your whole life now is proving of His power to enable you to do anything. You will never be able to fear again, I think, after all of this.[1]

The Bounce-Back Factor

One of the ways we learn to bounce back or be resilient is to look at people who have already done it. If you are surrounded by friends and family members who are laid low by life's experiences, *you* can be laid low just by breathing their air. Failure to be resilient can be catching because it is easy to see the compensations of staying down. Sympathy, pity, attention, notoriety, and excuses to bow out of what you do not want to do can be good "reasons" for not bouncing back.

When I was a kid, I loved to stay home from church for any reason. I do not know why, but any excuse was good enough for me. I had no reason to be resilient because there was no payoff. I did not want to go to church, so getting up and going had no appeal. However, when I was an older teenager, I worked at a favorite camp, surrounded by people and activities I loved. I had an appendicitis attack that led to surgery, a brief stay in the hospital, and a return to camp.

> If you are surrounded by friends and family members who are laid low by life's experiences, you can be laid low just by breathing their air.

Resilience was all over me then. All I wanted to do was recover and get back in the game. There was no way I was going to stay down. I probably should have gone home to recuperate because I had some tenuous days. I found that my desire to be involved, however, was greater than my physical limitations. I *wanted* to bounce back. I *wanted* resilience, so I had it.

That is a huge factor. To live with resilience, you have to *want* it. It may be in small matters or large, but bouncing back, going on to write new chapters and new stories, is primary. The payoff for being resilient has to be greater than the payoff for staying down or staying put. Sometimes you even have to *wait* to see what the payoff is while you are pushing on to bounce back. When you cannot see it clearly, it is a total leap of faith. Resilience can be its own reward.

Looking for a Way Out

Deb is a woman of passion and excellence, who found herself looking for a way out so she could bounce back. That may be where you are right now. (So many people are finding themselves without jobs or facing situations where it feels as if there is no place to go.) If so, you may appreciate her account of where she found herself and how she learned resilience. These are her words:

> There are times in life when you need to listen, really listen to the nudges of the Holy Spirit. It takes a lot of courage and wisdom if the nudges are about a complete career change and a leap into the unknown. This is particularly true if you are a type A multitasker as I am.
>
> I had a significant role as a director of operations in a large multifaceted church. In the initial stages, I embraced it wholeheartedly. I loved being busy, goal oriented, and focused on tasks that accomplished some meaningful outcomes. Over time, the tasks grew larger and longer. The job was taking a toll on me physically, emotionally, and mentally. I kept thinking, *But I'm in ministry; I have to keep doing this if I want to please God.* Eventually I hit a wall. Physically I was exhausted, and I was emotionally drained. I remember being in the grocery

store and almost in tears, pushing the cart and thinking, *What am I doing?*

All this time I could feel these nudges that were telling me to resign, but every time I tried, someone would say, "You don't want to do that. You're doing a great job." Finally, I got the message from the Lord that it would be easier if I took myself out rather than hang around until He had to pry my fingers loose.

So I resigned and woke up the next day, after a Thanksgiving weekend, wondering, *What have I done?* I was relieved, confused, and exhausted. I felt like a complete failure. I kept thinking about those I had left behind in ministry and my reputation for getting the job done. Then, I began to hear that question no type A wants to hear herself ask, *What do I do next?* I had no purpose, no strategic plan, and I had never learned how to be still.

It was a process that took over six months for me to be quiet enough to learn that I needed to be still, listen, and wait. Sometimes painful silence filled the room, and yet I had to realize that this was a different chapter in my life. The past was not coming back, and you can't go back and reclaim it. You either can stay stuck or you can move on. I learned that although I have no title or profession, I still am significant in the eyes of my Father. I still have purpose, wisdom, courage, and strength for the next step.

I have learned that resiliency comes from knowing that God's nature does not change according to my circumstances in life. He is always a good God and will always lead me to the next chapter of my story if I learn to wait on Him and His hand-print on the day-to-day experiences. This allowed me to regain my strength, to smile, and to laugh again. Yes, it takes time, not always just days or weeks, but sometimes it takes months or years. I no longer push doors open to know what is next, but instead, I wait on Him to provide me with exactly what I need.

It will be two years this fall since I resigned, and I have absolutely no regrets. I am stronger, happier, and more confident in who I am as an individual. The next chapter is being written. I don't know exactly where it will lead, but I do have direction and purpose. Resiliency is a gift and a choice. I am taking ownership for the next chapter myself and giving Him the glory for what lies ahead.

There are times when we have no power over the story into which we are cast, but we can make one choice—we can decide how to live. In the sovereign plan of God, there is meaning even in the difficult things that happen and in the things in which we have absolutely no choice.

Naaman's Servant Girl

A recorded incident in 2 Kings 5 tells of a little girl who had been kidnapped from her home in Israel and taken to Syria. She had no control over what happened to her, but she did make a decision about how she would conduct herself. Look at these few verses that tell the tale of a mighty commander and this little girl:

> Naaman was commander of the army of the king of Aram. He was honored by his master, and he had much respect because the LORD used him to give victory to Aram. He was a mighty and brave man, but he had a skin disease.

The Arameans had gone out to raid the Israelites and had taken a little girl as a captive. This little girl served Naaman's wife. She said to her mistress, "I wish my master would meet the prophet who lives in Samaria. He would cure him of his disease."

Naaman went to the king and told him what the girl from Israel had said. (vv. 1–4)

Can you think of a more traumatic situation for a child? A little girl was snatched from her homeland and taken to live in a totally different culture. She was placed in the great commander's house as a servant to his wife. One day she was a little Israelite girl living in a family, learning the ways of Yahweh. The next day she was a captive in a foreign land and servant to a woman of privilege. Can you imagine the mind-altering nature of that experience? Her story was written *for* her. What could she do? How could she change things?

The great commander, in whose house she was a servant, had a skin disease that he could not conquer. No doubt this was a matter of great concern and worry in the household. What a sweet picture to see this little girl in her childlike innocence go to her mistress and tell her that she wished Mr. Naaman could go to the prophet in Samaria, and he would be healed.

Naaman was probably desperate because as soon as he heard what the little Israelite girl had said to his wife, he went straight to the king and told him where he wanted to go and why. The king thought it was a good idea. (It was one of those times when people say, "You might as well go. You've tried everything else.") The king was so much in favor of it that he wrote a letter to the king of Israel and sent it by Naaman. With gold and silver in hand, Naaman headed out to Israel with the king's letter stating, "I am sending my servant Naaman to you so you can heal him of his skin disease" (v. 6).

Wait a minute. Who said the king of Israel could heal Naaman of his disease? That was not what the little servant girl had said, but somehow the story had been twisted—but that will be a discussion for a little later in this chapter, and we will see a new narrative begin.

Silver Linings

My friend June Scobee Rodgers is a woman who understands how you can be in one place one minute and the next find yourself catapulted someplace else. On a cold January 28, 1986, she, along with her children, watched as her pilot husband, Dick Scobee, met his tragic death. He was the commander of the Space Shuttle *Challenger* that had just lifted off the launch pad when it exploded in midair right in front of his wife, family, and the whole nation. (This was the flight the first teacher in space, Christa McAuliffe, was on, and millions of school children were also watching from their classrooms.) June tells about the historic, fateful moment in her own words:

> We watched in silence as our loved ones climbed the sky sunward. Their craft from the distance seemed to sit atop a great flume of smoke. The floor shook with the sheer raw power of the millions of pounds of thrust . . . My son lovingly and protectively put his arms around his sister and me. As I reached to help my daughter Kathie with the baby, it happened! The

unspeakable happened. Standing there together, watching with all the world, we saw the shuttle rip apart. The SRBs went screaming off on their own separate paths, and the orbiter with our loved ones exploded in the cold blue sky, and like our hearts, it shattered into a million pieces.[2]

The unthinkable happened. Hopes, dreams, plans, and lives were radically changed in one horrifying moment. The story June Scobee was living had come to an unexpected halt. She was numb and in shock, but what could she do now? What would happen? Would she survive, or did her shattered heart mean that her life was over?

June Scobee had a choice: she could crawl into a lonely hole of silence and grief, or she could move through the next days, months, and years with hope that, despite the shattering of the dream she once had known, she could go on. June moved from being the devastated victim of a horrific accident that took the love of her life to being the victor who was learning lessons that helped her grow, change, and bloom.

In her book, *Silver Linings*, June wrote,

What lessons have I learned? I've learned, as Matthew Arnold expressed it, "to see life steadily and to see it whole." I've learned that beauty in life and happiness are not found in the controlled, forced environment of my doing, but in the joy of experiencing life freely, naturally, without the clutter of anger, envy, fear, or guilt that stifles and bogs down our lives. It is found in the sheer sweet pleasure and joy of experiencing life at its fullest and most pleasurable moments.

I've learned that when one door is closed, God opens another. To close the door on yesterday allows the door of today to swing open more fully. Dwelling on what was or might-have-been steals from us what is today or can be tomorrow.[3]

After *Challenger* exploded, June discovered that God still had plans and good surprises for her life. She made the choice to go on, to write new chapters, now as the widow of Commander Dick Scobee. She kept his dream of exploring space alive by helping to create the Challenger Centers that offer students all over America a different kind of field trip—"a field trip outside the boundaries of our planet." Students come to the centers to learn teamwork, communication, problem solving, and critical thinking in a high-tech environment that gives them an experience in simulated space travel.

> "To close the door on yesterday allows the door of today to swing open more fully."

God had another surprise waiting for June as well. She met Lieutenant General Don Rodgers, who, like June, was finding his way back from a personal explosion. His wife of thirty-two years had died suddenly and left him a widower. As only God can do in His providence, He brought June and Don together to find a new life that neither of them ever knew was possible. They married and June wrote, "That day I discovered joy as great as my sorrow had been deep. God blessed me with another chance to love and be loved, but more important was my rekindled spirit."[4]

Having a *rekindled spirit* is the heart of resilience. Learning the art of bouncing back is a requirement for writing a new story. The old story can only last so long, and then it begins to grow stale, holding us back with the ghost of what-was always lurking in the background. It becomes a choice—a choice to look at what-can-be rather than what-might-have-been.

No doubt you have heard the quote, "Perspective is everything." And, indeed, it is! Life happens with all of its highs, lows, and everything between, but that is not what matters. It is your view of life that matters. How do you interpret circumstances? Do you see them as stumbling blocks or stepping-stones? One view keeps you where you are. The other basically allows you to use the stones as springboards to whatever is next. Good perspective sees what's next as an adventure. Negative perspective sees the next thing as another potential disappointment.

Columnist and author Anna Quindlen writes about her perspective in *A Short Guide to a Happy Life*. After something bad happened to her (which she never describes), she learned to really live. She counsels, "And think of life as a terminal illness, because, if you do, you will live it with joy and passion, as it ought to be lived."[5]

Writing a new story can be described as learning to live life in a new way. It is taking a different look, holding it up to the light to see different colors, and maybe even putting a different spin on things than you have in the past.

Reframing

A popular word that crops up in many contexts today is *reframing*. It means that you take a second look and rearrange the way you see something. For instance, if you sprain your ankle and see it as an awful inconvenience, you can reframe the experience and see it as a chance to move through life at a slower pace. Instead of being your usual antsy self about the slower pace, you can reframe it and look at it as an opportunity to pay attention to some of the things around you that you have been missing. As you pay closer attention, you may decide to reframe your response to some little things that have far more import than you have been willing to give them.

When it is time to move on, it is often the reframing of something in your world that creates the power to do it. That is why it is possible to have the same life but write a new story—one that springs out of your choice to be resilient and to bounce back. If you find yourself stuck, why not think through how you can go about reframing your view of your situation?

Do you think maybe that was what Jesus was suggesting to us when He said to look at the birds and the flowers and think about how faithful our heavenly Father is to take care of them? Was He teaching us to reframe our thinking? He was asking us to notice that the birds and flowers do not go lacking, so why should we worry about doing without food and clothing? He pointed out that the birds always eat, and the flowers' clothing is more beautiful than royals' finery.

Look at the birds in the air. They don't plant or harvest or store food in barns, but your heavenly Father feeds them. And you know that you are worth much more than the birds. You cannot add any time to your life by worrying about it.

And why do you worry about clothes? Look at how the lilies in the field grow. They don't work or make clothes for themselves. But I tell you that even Solomon with his riches was not dressed as beautifully as one of these flowers. . . . Seek first God's kingdom and what God wants. Then all your other needs will be met as well. So don't worry about tomorrow, because tomorrow will have its own worries. Each day has enough trouble of its own. (Matt. 6:26–29, 33–34)

In other words, *reframe* the way you see these necessities of life, take a look around you and see how the birds and flowers do under God's care, and then decide how you will make it by trusting Him. That is reframing. You can worry yourself silly about issues in your life, but it does not change a thing. You cannot add a day to your life or an inch to your height.

Jesus was redirecting His disciples' attention to another way of seeing life and, consequently, another way of living. Instead of focusing on their needs and how they were going to get them met, He told them to reframe their whole approach to the issue. Since God knew they needed those things, they could shift their emphasis. In fact, they could rewrite a whole life script. Seek God and His kingdom first, and God would take care of all the smaller issues that held their focus.

That is the picture of bouncing back from navel gazing and worry. Jesus said, in effect, "Stop writing a story in your life about all the needs that seem insurmountable. Reframe it. Take God at His Word. If God says He'll take care of you, then why not live as though that were true?"

How you write your story is up to you. You do not get to decide on the circumstances for the most part, but you do get to decide what you will do about the circumstances. Dr. Dan Baker relates an event in his book *What Happy People Know* that describes this whole concept in a lovely way.

He tells about two women who came into his office. They both were young, well educated, and financially secure. They both had problems that were bothersome to them: one had cancer, and the other had pimples.

The young woman with cancer had also recently lost her husband in a car wreck. Dr. Baker thought she would want to talk about her grief and fear. Instead, she claimed to be a lucky young woman. She had survived the wreck, had money to get the best treatment, had time to take off from work, her cancer survival rate was favorable, and she felt blessed to have had her husband for as long as she did.

She related the events of her life in a true and healthy way. She was not a Pollyanna. She got it. Reality is reality, and she had a plan for bouncing back and moving on. The past was just that, so she planned to move on to a new future.

The other young woman he saw in his office had a moderate case of acne. No scarring or pitting. Just some dots of pimples here and there that she concealed with makeup.

She told a completely different tale. She was undone. She saw herself as a monster, and the saga she told was of a life with no hope of love and the fear of dying alone. The more she talked about it, the more she believed it, and Dr. Baker said when she left the office after an hour, "I was seeing a lot more acne than when she arrived."[6]

The power of the story you tell is beyond belief. You can talk yourself in and out of being resilient. If you decide to bounce back, you will. If you believe resilience is not available to you, then you will buy the helplessness that comes along with such an account. You can be trapped in a situation solely because that is the way you tell your story.

Resilience Has a Ring to It

People with resilience and the power to bounce back typically have similar characteristics:

Creativity. People who can bounce back will take a creative approach toward dealing with things that are painful and hard to handle. They do not see themselves as stuck. They will reject the thought that they have no hope or way to reframe their circumstances. They know that if they back themselves into a corner of no hope they truly are stuck.

Persistence. Those persons who want to write a new story will be persistent in finding what has to happen to move on. They have a certain independent tenacity that says, "No is not an answer," and, "I *will* find how to turn this thing around."

Ability to let go. When you are trying to reach for something just beyond your grasp, it is imperative to let go of what you are carrying in your hand. You have to come to new solutions and new stories empty-handed—willing to release the old ways of thinking and doing things.

Curiosity. Resilient people have a strong curiosity about new ways of doing things and new ways of thinking. The least resilient people, who will likely never bounce back, are those who are complacent and satisfied with the way things are and with what they already know. A vibrant curiosity will keep you open to what might be waiting right around the corner.

Sense of humor. You may not be a natural wit, but everyone can learn to laugh, and laughter is a huge part of reframing or bouncing back. If you cannot laugh about some of the absurdities of life, then you are going to take what happens much too seriously and find yourself stuck.

As I mentioned, going through my father's last years was a horrendous experience for my mother and for me. His dementia tore him away, and there was a whole part of who I was that had to learn to cope and move on after that experience, but we did have times of laughter—and what a relief they were. The crazy thing is that the laughter was all wrapped up in the disease.

My dad had always been a natural wit with an incredible sense of timing. He made people laugh wherever we went, and if I have a sense of humor today, it is because I inherited it from him.

When he was sick and his mind was not working as well, all kinds of bizarre things happened. From time to time, I just had to laugh. He no longer had his sense of humor, so if anyone was smiling, it had to be me.

Dad's physical therapist, a darling little female, came by one day to see him. He was confined to his hospital bed. One of the exercises she did with him required her to climb up in the bed to rearrange some overhead equipment. I was in the room reading and looked up when I heard him protesting loudly. He did not want the young therapist to climb up on his bed. He was waving his hand, saying, "No. No."

I said, "What's wrong, Daddy?"

He began to spell out a word: *e-t-h-i-c-s*. I had to smile because he could not carry on a straight conversation, much less spell abstract words, but on that day, he did.

I said, "You don't want her to climb on the side of the bed because it's wrong?"

He said, "Yes, ethics."

So I told the young lady she would have to find another way to do the exercises because she was violating his ethics. We both chuckled and shrugged. The whole thing was bizarre and a little funny right in the middle of the sadness of it all. However, it became part of the process that enabled me to bounce back from my old story and move on. There were some funny moments, and honestly, if I remember anything from those awful days, I really do remember the things that made us laugh.

Resilience or bouncing back is *intentional*. It doesn't just happen, particularly after really hard times. Just as writing a new story has to be intentional, so the resilience it takes to get there is a choice. Some days it will seem like a lot of work, but mostly it is choosing to do what you can and trusting God with the rest, with a grateful heart. That combination works in many ways and circumstances.

A Little Girl with Big News

The life of one Israelite child, known to us only as the little girl who waited on Naaman's wife, paints a stunning picture of resilience amidst unspeakable circumstances.

In her new situation, Naaman was the one she considered her master. He was the head of the house and husband to her mistress. Although he was a very successful military man, he probably walked around the house frustrated and unhappy because he had a skin disease. Since most men do not make the best patients, he probably let everyone in earshot know how disgruntled he was about his skin. The little girl could not help but notice. We do not know how old she was, but I can imagine her processing this whole scenario in her little head and then quietly approaching her mistress with the news that she knew a place where Naaman could get some relief. Once Mrs. Naaman told him what the little girl had said, he immediately went to the king and told him he wanted to go south and find help.

Let's pick up the story in 2 Kings 5:5–7:

> So Naaman left and took with him about seven hundred fifty pounds of silver, as well as one hundred fifty pounds of gold and ten changes of clothes. He brought the letter to the king of Israel, which read, "I am sending my servant Naaman to you so you can heal him of his skin disease."
>
> When the king of Israel read the letter, he tore his clothes to show how upset he was. He said, "I'm not God! I can't kill and make alive again! Why does this man send someone with a skin disease for me to heal? You can see that the king of Aram is trying to start trouble with me."

Whoa! The king of Israel, flabbergasted by Naaman's expectation, said, "Wait a minute! Who told you I could heal your skin disease? Who am I, God? You are terribly mistaken—I can't do this."

Word about the king's outrage spread quickly. There is something about a mad king that is a little disconcerting to most people, but not to the prophet of God.

> When Elisha, the man of God, heard that the king of Israel had torn his clothes, he sent the king this message: "Why have you torn your clothes? Let Naaman come to me. Then he will know there is a prophet in Israel." So Naaman went with his horses and chariots to Elisha's house and stood outside the door.
>
> Elisha sent Naaman a messenger who said, "Go and wash

in the Jordan River seven times. Then your skin will be healed, and you will be clean."

Naaman became angry and left. He said, "I thought Elisha would surely come out and stand before me and call on the name of the LORD his God. I thought he would wave his hand over the place and heal the disease. The Abana and the Pharpar, the rivers of Damascus, are better than all the waters of Israel. Why can't I wash in them and become clean?" So Naaman went away very angry. (vv. 8–12)

It is interesting to me that Naaman, who had been suffering with the skin disease evidently for a long time, was still so arrogant that he was willing to *keep* the disease in order to get his ego stroked. He preferred to stay in his old, diseased story, rather than take a simple action to move on to a new, disease-free story. And then I think, *How many times have I acted that way too?* Sigh. Can you imagine how tired God must get of our arrogance and inertia? Let's see how He moved Naaman from arrogant to humble:

Naaman's servants came near and said to him, "My father, if the prophet had told you to do some great thing, wouldn't you have done it? Doesn't it make more sense just to do it? After all, he only told you, 'Wash, and you will be clean.'" So Naaman went down and dipped in the Jordan seven times, just as Elisha had said. Then his skin became new again, like the skin of a child. And he was clean. (vv. 13–14)

Just do it, Naaman, just do it! Oh, how often we need to just do what the Lord tells us to do. No excuses. No false expectations. No arrogance. Just humble obedience. *Then* we can bounce back and move forward. When it occurred to Naaman that he would have to humble himself or stay diseased, he went back to see Elisha:

> Naaman and all his group returned to Elisha. He stood before Elisha and said, "Look, I now know there is no God in all the earth except in Israel. Now please accept a gift from me."
>
> But Elisha said, "As surely as the LORD lives whom I serve, I won't accept anything." Naaman urged him to take the gift, but he refused.
>
> Then Naaman said, "If you won't take the gift, then please give me some soil—as much as two of my mules can carry. From now on I'll not offer any burnt offering or sacrifice to any other gods but the LORD. But let the LORD pardon me for this: When my master goes into the temple of Rimmon to worship, he leans on my arm. Then I must bow in that temple. May the LORD pardon me when I do that."
>
> Elisha said to him, "Go in peace." (vv. 15–19)

Wow! What an about-face for Naaman. On the spot he discarded his arrogance (a form of self-worship) and the worship of other false gods (Rimmon), and he created a new way of living in which he promised never to worship any other god again except the true God of Israel. So in addition to owing the little servant girl his gratitude for saving his physical life, he owed her a greater debt of gratitude for his new eternal life with God. *That's* what you call a great new story!

Jesus even mentioned Naaman's story in Luke 4:27: "There were many with skin diseases living in Israel during the time of the prophet Elisha. But none of them were healed, only Naaman, who was from the country of Syria." So not only was Naaman healed by God, but he was also the *only one* healed at that time.

The *Instead* Option

The little girl from Israel, stolen from her homeland and forced into servitude to an arrogant man's wife in a foreign country, could have easily wished for Naaman's skin disease to eat through his fingers and toes. She could have remained focused on her misfortune and festered with resentment and hatred. Many people would in her circumstances.

Instead, she wished for his cure. *Instead*, she spoke up when silence would have probably been an easier choice. *Instead*, she provided the means for him to be cured. *Instead*, she led him to God and eternal life. *Instead*, she chose to write a new story with her own life. *Instead*, even when no one else was being healed, she chose to believe that God would heal her master.

When life's circumstances are tough, an *instead* option is always available. It is up to us to choose the *instead*, rather than the status quo, in order to turn our stories to new pages of hope and joy.

Personal Reflection

1. If you had been the one stolen from your family and home, how do you think you would have felt? Why?
2. Have you ever been in a position where you could have wished evil on someone who hurt you? Describe.
3. Tell of a time when you helped someone find his/her way to God and create a new story.
4. Describe a time when you had to choose between hurting or helping someone. What choice did you make?
5. Are you in a place in your life now from which you need to bounce back and move forward? Explain.
6. How can you apply the *instead* option to help you write your new story?

Journal Entry

To continue your new story, complete the following starter sentence in your personal journal. Then continue writing thoughts and feelings from your heart as long as you need to.

I really want to bounce back from my old story and spring forward into a new story, and to do that I know I need to apply the instead *option to . . .*

Group Discussion Questions

1. If you could write a short list of contrasts between Naaman and the little girl, what would you put on the list?

2. What misunderstanding did Naaman have with the king of Israel?

3. How did Naaman eventually end up at Elisha's house?

4. Since Naaman seemed to do everything in a big way, describe the scene as you imagine it happened when he arrived on the prophet's front lawn.

5. What were Naaman's preconceived ideas about how he should be healed? Why do you think he had those ideas?

6. What basis did the little girl have for believing Elisha could heal her master? Explain.

7. When the prophet did not do things Naaman's way, what did he tell Elisha he had expected?

8. What was Naaman's personal characteristic that reared its ugly head?

9. How was Naaman eventually healed? And what truth did Naaman learn about God?

10. How did Naaman say that truth about God would change his life story?

11. Whose initial influence put Naaman in the position to learn about and believe in God?

12. What overarching principles can you draw from this story? And how do they apply to us today?

Chapter 10

THE LAST CHAPTER
HAS NOT BEEN
WRITTEN YET!

Once, while St. Francis of Assisi was hoeing his garden, he was asked, "What would you do if you were suddenly to learn that you were to die at sunset today?" He replied, "I would finish hoeing my garden."

Elizabeth

Elizabeth lived a story in her last days she
never dreamed she would live, finishing well
and leaving a powerful legacy.

LUKE 1:5–80

Elizabeth thought she was living peacefully in the final chapters of her old story. She thought her life was nearly over. She and her husband, Zechariah, were elderly, and they had never had any children. Probably the last thing on her mind was getting pregnant.

Then God's angel, Gabriel, paid a visit to Zechariah while he was serving in the temple. He came to tell Zechariah that Elizabeth was going to have a baby. While Zechariah was struck dumb by the news, Elizabeth seemed to take it in stride. And at the given time, John was born.

When he grew up, John was no ordinary man. He was, in fact, perhaps one of the most important men who had ever been born up to that time. God appointed him to an extremely significant calling. And it was through her unexpected son, John, that Elizabeth's legacy is remembered today, as you will soon see.

W hen the letter came saying Melda was moving to assisted living in another state, my heart cried. Melda and Sarah have been close friends for seventy years. Now, because their family members live in different states, they will have to live in separate assisted living facilities many miles apart. Each of them has to make a hard decision because Melda and Sarah no longer can care for themselves. They know that when they say good-bye this time, they probably will not see one another again on this earth. And so a new story begins. This is not a story either of them would *choose* to write, but it is a story that *must* be written.

Often we find ourselves staring at the first page of a story we would not have chosen to write, but because we are still breathing, the story must be told. As long as we live, we will write. Even in the last chapters of life, there are sweet scenes and precious scenarios that can be recorded. The important thing to remember is, even in these days, what we write is important, and the messages God wants to deliver through us will be remembered, perhaps by people we do not even know.

By the time you get to the last chapters of your life, you will realize some things that you may never have considered before:

- Time is of the essence.
- The stories that matter most are not necessarily the really big ones.

- While you breathe you still have something to write.
- Your story will be told whether it is good or bad.

Recently I heard a young woman say, "I'm in my thirties now, you know." She said it as if she wanted to add, "So I have to take some things into account I haven't had to think about before." I had to giggle because I have finished my second set of thirties, and I have to consider some different things too! Mostly, I think time is more important to me now. I no longer think about preparation for the future because I am living my future. I am writing some of my finishing chapters, and I want to write them well, but if I waste my days, I have only myself to blame for an unwritten legacy. Who will communicate what I want to say? If I want to write, I have to do it and so do you.

I wonder, if we left this earth tomorrow, what stories would those who love us remember?

- Are we fun?
- Are we wise?
- Are we self-centered?
- Are we high-maintenance?
- Are we flexible?
- Are we generous?
- Are we _____? (You can fill in the blank.)

We cannot control our circumstances, but we *can* control how we respond to the circumstances even as we grow older and even as we move to a stage of life that may seem as if we are losing control. Sometimes the last chapters are hard to write. When your strength diminishes and your passions wane, it can be difficult to think of purposefully writing a story that matters. Finishing well is usually the theme of the story, and yet finishing well is not always as easy to write about as it may seem.

The Undone

When you are writing your last chapters, you probably will be aware that some things have been left undone. It is not so much about the *things to do* as it is about the *person you wanted to become.* That is the person who will write your last chapters. You may think, *But I wanted to do and be so much more.* The good news is that you can do just that, if you want to. God has uniquely created us to increase in awareness and wisdom as we grow older. That wisdom is what comes from suffering, hard times, and things in life we did not necessarily appreciate at the time. In fact, God has created our brains to continue growing and increasing in wisdom as we lean into our strengths and make the effort to live intentionally.

I love the new information we are learning about the *neuroplasticity* of the brain. That big word just means that our adaptable brains continue to grow and change as long as we live. We are not stuck even when we are writing the last chapters of our lives.

Brain cells start out with maybe only one connection, called a *dendrite*, but, if over the course of time, the brain is nourished well and stimulated by learning, both good and bad, it can grow new connections (dendrites) that, in turn, make connections with other cells. Now this is the interesting part for our last-chapter years. This process can take a long time. During your lifetime, a dendrite might send out four, five, or six branches. (You may say, "So?" but trust me; this is so good.)

The first five branches are basically identical. But the sixth branch or side is remarkable. Unlike the first five, it has the amazing ability to keep growing. It can explore and seek out new connections on its own. When this occurs, it creates the ultimate brain cell, capable of finding knowledge that is out of the reach of lesser cells.

Often the knowledge is not straightforward, factual knowledge, such as one plus one equals two. Ordinary brain cells can figure that out. Instead, it is knowledge about the meaning, significance, and connection of facts. It is the highest form of knowledge: wisdom.

Think on that one for a minute, and then consider this: in a study done by Walter Bortz, MD, at Stanford University, wisdom is the "best single predictor of aging well."[1]

What does that mean to us? Our *last* chapters can be the *best* chapters because our brains have connected, that wisdom dendrite is growing, and our understanding is becoming more and more insightful. We can see deeper into the issues of life and become writers of stories that bless others because of the way we have been blessed to understand. It is an amazing thing to be given something you know you could not conjure up on your own, yet you know it is an intrinsic part of who you are. Only God can give wisdom. No book, no scholar, no great thinker can put it into your brain. Only God can do that. These words from Proverbs 3 state it so well. The wisdom of the years is a gift, and it often comes with age.

> *Blessed is the man who finds wisdom,*
> *the man who gains understanding,*
> *for she is more profitable than silver*
> *and yields better returns than gold . . .*

Long life is in her right hand;
in her left hand are riches and honor . . .
She is a tree of life to those who embrace her;
those who lay hold of her will be blessed.
(13–14, 16, 18 NIV)

Finishing Well

Alexandra Goode is a wise woman who is finishing well. She is a woman who has written what most of us would consider four or five full-length novels with her life. She was orphaned during the horrific days of World War II. Her privileged life with a loving family turned into the nightmarish existence of an abandoned orphan in wartime. Through an unbelievable set of circumstances, Alexandra found herself in a Nazi concentration camp, but because of the unseen hand that held the pen, she was preserved.

Alexandra was able to immigrate to the United States where she met a young naval lieutenant, George Goode, and began a new life as wife and mother.

Now in her final chapters, she is as full of life and determination as she was in the days when she was trying just to survive another day. Today she is rescuing orphans from eastern Europe. She does not take care of just those who are healthy, cute, and adoptable, but she seeks out the children who are too old to be wanted or who have physical challenges that keep them from finding adoptive parents. Through their organization, International Guardian Angels Outreach (igao.org), she and George continue to see the incredible and impossible happen.

Just this past year Alexandra and George traveled to Russia one more time to pick up two special needs children. One of the children they brought back was a precious little five-year-old girl with a visible birth defect. At a time when most people their ages are trying to decide which retirement community to go into, George and Alexandra were seeking God for a doctor and foster parents to take care of a disabled little girl from an orphanage halfway around the world. They found both by God's clear direction, and she has now had her third surgery. She is also with a family who treats her as their own loved child.

The Goodes are writing their last chapters with an eye toward continuing their work through their children and grandchildren. Some child not yet born in Russia will end up in an orphanage and need surgery. Because of the passion of Alexandra and George, help will be available. Today they are making provision for some little one not yet born. What more meaningful story could they write?

The Hands of Jesus

Frances is another storywriter who understands the unseen hand and the essence of time. She is a slight woman who works as a senior personal trainer and swimming instructor. She has a shy, winning smile that reveals a heart touched by God, literally. She is another one who has lived enough life to fill three or four full-length books.

Frances's first years were chaotic and unbridled. She grew up as one of six kids in a family where abuse was an everyday part of life. She ran from that unholy scene to the sadness of having a baby she was forced to put up for adoption. She then started a new life with a man who promised to love her but, instead, became her worst nightmare. His "love" led her to drugs, prostitution, and time in jail.

Somewhere in the chapters of her chaotic, dysfunctional life, Frances aborted a child she never would see, and then she gave birth to a child she kept and reared to manhood. She loved him and tried to be a good mother. She gave him all she knew and all she could give. Her longing for a fuller, more complete life never left her.

The men in Frances's world failed her, but surely, she thought, *I can find a God who is bigger than the men who have failed me.* Her search led her to a cult where they groomed her to be a minister. She embraced the teaching with a probing zeal, but something still was not right. She finally left the cult and moved on.

Then Frances found herself in an unlikely southern city, working at a sports facility. After being there for a while, she experienced some disturbing symptoms and discovered she had a brain tumor. After it was successfully removed, she returned to her work, grateful to be well but still with a deep longing for something she could not seem to find.

One night Frances had an encounter that totally changed her life. God spoke to her in her sleep. He explained everything she needed to know about Him. Sounds implausible, right? But He must have done it because Fran went to bed with questions, and the next morning she had answers. She awoke to discover that she was a new creature—old things had passed away, and all things had become new (2 Cor. 5:17). She had met her most intimate, loving Friend, Jesus. Her new story was beginning. She knew she had to find a place where there were other people who knew this God she had just met. She did not want to just look in the Yellow Pages, so she decided to ask someone she knew and had watched.

Frances went to a swim class she taught and asked a student she thought might be a Christian where she attended church. The woman was dumbfounded because she had been praying about how to invite Frances to church. She had felt God pull on her to ask her, but she just was not sure how to go about it. Frances and God beat her to it.

Frances went to the church, got involved in every class that would challenge her brain, and found a peace she never had known. Then her story took another turn. She joined a group of women who had come out of extremely challenging lives, and they began ministering to people living on the streets. Weekly they took them food, blankets, and the good news that God knew where they were and He loved them.

She had met her most intimate, loving Friend, Jesus. Her new story was beginning.

That was not enough for Frances, though. She believed God wanted her to do more and to be prepared to do it when the need arose. So she packed the trunk of her car with blankets, clean clothes, bottles of water, and food. She did not know how God would write her new story as she pulled all the elements together and stored them for the opportunity she knew would come.

The very day she prayed, "God, You'll just have to bring the people to me," she walked right into a homeless couple. The man was aimlessly pushing a wheelchair with a woman in it, who had vomited on herself and was sitting in her own excrement.

When Frances saw them, she sensed the Lord saying, "Now, Frances."

So she stopped them, talked with them, and told them she would help. She ran to her car and got the clean clothes, a blanket, and some water, and then she led them to a nearby public restroom where she stood guard while the man took the woman in and cleaned her up. The woman emerged, wiped down from her filth and wearing fresh clothes that Frances just happened to have in her car. The old, vile clothes were thrown away. They both thanked her profusely and then went on their way.

Frances never saw them again, but for that moment, she knew she had been the hands of Jesus to them. That is her new story. She is the hands of Jesus to people who have no way to use their hands and some who have no hands. This is one of the final books in her library of incredible stories. No one can predict how it all will end, but this much we know—God is the ultimate Author, and Frances is a cooperative character in a story that could have abruptly ended more than once in so many awful ways.

God is the Author who writes our stories, and we are the characters who choose to live out our parts in His drama.

Both Frances and Alexandra recognized that life is not forever. We must live the days we are assigned, not the days in the future we do not have yet. They both have discovered that giving to others keeps them vibrant and full of the delight of living the adventures God has given them today.

There is a real paradox to living the same life and writing a new story. God is the Author who writes our stories, and we are the characters who choose to live out our parts in His drama. Either we do it with delight and the faith to believe that He knows what He is doing, or we do it in fear and rebellion, convinced that we know a better way. Our own perspectives determine the ultimate outcomes of the stories—how they are told, how they look, and how they impact others.

Elizabeth's Last Chapter?

Elizabeth, who lived at the time of Jesus, knew this. She came from a long line of priests, who were descended from Aaron. She loved the Lord, and it is recorded in the Scriptures that she "truly did what God said was good" (Luke 1:5). So did her husband, Zechariah. They had lived a lot of years together; Scripture tells us they were both very old, but they had not been blessed with children. They were in their last chapters, so the thought of children was probably no longer in their thinking. (In that time, to have children was a sign of blessing and God's approval. Barrenness is always an issue to be reckoned with, but in that environment, it was particularly so.)

Zechariah was from a priestly line as well, so he did a lot of service in the temple. Let's connect with him there because his backstory fits right into Elizabeth's script. This is such an endearing account that has ultimately impacted us all. Put yourself in Zechariah's shoes as he gets the news that his world is about to change. He was serving in the temple where, by lot, he had been chosen to go. He was performing his duty of burning incense when the angel of the Lord appeared to him.

> When he saw the angel, Zechariah was startled and frightened. But the angel said to him, "Zechariah, don't be afraid. God has heard your prayer. Your wife, Elizabeth, will give birth to a son, and you will name him John. He will bring you

joy and gladness, and many people will be happy because of his birth. John will be a great man for the Lord. He will never drink wine or beer, and even from birth, he will be filled with the Holy Spirit. He will help many people of Israel return to the Lord their God. He will go before the Lord in spirit and power like Elijah. He will make peace between parents and their children and will bring those who are not obeying God back to the right way of thinking, to make a people ready for the coming of the Lord."

Zechariah said to the angel, "How can I know that what you say is true? I am an old man, and my wife is old, too." (Luke 1:12–18)

Zechariah probably realized that time was short; he was not young, nor was Elizabeth. Could it be the angel had arrived at the wrong address and was giving this news to the wrong Zechariah? He had to ask, and the angel had to answer, "I am Gabriel. I stand before God, who sent me to talk to you and to tell you this good news" (v. 19).

Can you imagine the quaking of the old man's knees when the angel identified himself and repeated to him that God had sent him to give him the news? Doubt is tough. It sometimes can keep you from trouble when you doubt men, but when you doubt God, it is never a good idea. Just ask Zechariah, who learned the lesson the hard way as the angel continued speaking:

"Now, listen! You will not be able to speak until the day these things happen, because you did not believe what I told you. But they will really happen."

Outside, the people were still waiting for Zechariah and

were surprised that he was staying so long in the Temple. When Zechariah came outside, he could not speak to them, and they knew he had seen a vision in the Temple. He could only make signs to them and remained unable to speak. When his time of service at the Temple was finished, he went home. (vv. 20–23)

And guess who was waiting. Yes, our Elizabeth. We will join her later, but remember all of this news was happening to an old man and old woman, who thought they were about to live their latter years, hopefully in peace. When you finally come to the realization that time is of the essence, it is easier to quit questioning and relax into God's plan, whatever that might be.

Nell Mohney is one of those women who lives out her life confidently, resting in the greater story God has planned for her. She is a trim, always beautifully coifed woman in her last chapters. She is the widow of a wonderful pastor, who loved her supremely and died before she was ready to let him go. She also is the mother of two sons—one who died in a car accident long before his mother could have imagined she would have to say good-bye.

"We only go around once in life, and this is no dress rehearsal!"

Nell is in her last chapters now. She has lived her past well and now has lived up most of her future. Still, she is known for her wisdom, tenacity, grace, and service. She has not stopped or missed a beat in her story. She has not let self-pity, aging, or loneliness affect the account she is telling to all who will listen.

In our community, the name Nell Mohney is synonymous with fortitude, common sense, love of others, and godliness. Her story just keeps on keeping on at a time when many others her age are living humdrum stories, just waiting to die or win the lottery. Those who are waiting fail to take into account that we only get to do this life once, and time really is of the essence. As the old adage says, "We only go around once in life, and this is no dress rehearsal!"

Your Story Does Not Have to Be Big

Small tales make up memories that really matter. It does not have to be about big things, but it does take effort to tell even small stories. My paternal grandmother died when I was very young, and I never connected with her, but I heard that she was a loving woman. Although I did not know that from firsthand experience, what I did know was that she related that love to me before I was even born by making a quilt just for me.

Grandmother was very elderly when I was expected. My daddy was her late-life baby, and her other children and grandchildren were all much older. My dad married my mother and early on had to draw some strong boundaries with his mother because she did not want to let her baby boy go. She and my mother were not close because of that, so I have no idea what her thoughts toward me might have been, except she left a gift in the quilt she handmade for me. The quilt's design was repeated little girls with matching red bonnets. Each stitch of the quilting was clearly done with care.

I remember the quilt being in my room as I was growing up, but I did not know where it came from. By the time I was old enough to know she had made it for me, she was gone. I never got to thank her, but when I look at the quilt now, I hold it and think of that small sign she left for me that told me I had a grandmother who had thoughts of me.

No matter what page you are on in your life, if you have breath, you are still telling someone something. We are not blank slates. We are communicating. We cannot go back and change what was, but today we can recognize what is and determine to say what we really want said, not what we have just settled for in life. God has the big picture in mind while we live out the many lesser accounts told by what we think and how we view the circumstances of our lives.

A Matter of Life and Death

Sometimes we are called upon to tell a tale of life and death. Carole Harvey is a woman who came face to face with a choice about life or death in every area of her life. She was gracious enough to tell me her experience and allow me to share it with you. This is Carole's story:

Most of us pay attention when someone says, "This is a matter of life and death." My experience in June of 2002 was more a matter of "death and life," although I didn't know that was the story waiting for me.

My husband, Jim, and I were coming home to Little Rock from a visit with some of our family in Chattanooga. We had left before 5:00 a.m., so I was stretched out in the backseat of the car sound asleep. When we reached Nashville, Jim hit an oil slick on the road. The car swerved out of control and slammed into the railing on the side of the highway.

When the air bags went off, smoke began to fill the car. Jim opened my door in the back and said, "You've got to get out! I think the car is on fire!" I calmly said, "I don't think I can move." I wasn't in pain, yet I knew not to move. In a few minutes, paramedics appeared and put me on a backboard. What I believed was true. I couldn't move. My neck was broken.

My X-rays were seen by doctors in Little Rock and Nashville. The prediction from some was dire and sobering. They said I would die or be totally paralyzed. Others said the damage was great, but my losses would be only partial. Either way, I was in trouble. That was the story as they saw it and told it. Everything within me withered. The Scriptures tell us that we are made of body, soul, and spirit. The news I was given brought death to every one of those parts of me. I thought my life was over.

The surgeon put me in a "halo" brace for three months. It weighed fifteen pounds, and while I wore that heavy contraption, my weight plummeted to eighty-five pounds. I spent three weeks in the hospital in Nashville and then went home to the hospital in Little Rock on the Fourth of July (normally a celebratory day) for more recovery and physical therapy. The woman who came home to Little Rock was a broken shadow of the one who had left.

My left hand and arm were lifeless. The doctors couldn't tell me how much strength, if any, I would regain. I couldn't dress myself, brush my hair, or walk without a walker. I began to have unexplained blackouts and would go into a catatonic state. I dreamed I was dead, and I really believed I was! The head of the psychiatric unit was called in. After doing his tests, he pronounced that I had suffered brain damage and diagnosed me with early onset Alzheimer's disease. The Scriptures say in Proverbs 18:21, "The tongue has the power of life and death" (NIV), and indeed, that was true for me. I began to live out the doctor's diagnosis.

I was sent home to live or die; no one knew which it would be. As my physical condition improved, I deteriorated mentally. I was paralyzed internally with a spirit of fear. I had been released to drive, but I got lost on familiar streets. I made bad decisions driving as I fought with panic attacks. I went to the grocery store but would spend thirty minutes staring at products, unable to find what I wanted to buy, even though the item was right in front of me. At the library I would select a book, then I couldn't remember what to do next. I volunteered to read to a blind student, but I would get confused and read the wrong section. I tutored a fourth grader, but I couldn't remember what simple words meant. The confusion of it all led to a deep depression and sleeplessness.

Physical disability and mental death were closing in on me, but they were not the worst deaths. The worst of all was my spiritual death. In the past, I had enjoyed a close relationship with God. I knew He spoke to me and led me. Now the Scriptures had become just words, and God seemed silent to my cries.

I am a pianist, and I had enjoyed worshipping as I played spiritual songs and hymns, but I had no desire to touch the piano, even after regaining the use of my left hand. Many friends prayed for me and visited me, bringing me meals, thoughtful gifts, cards, and their presence. Nothing brought me comfort. I looked everywhere for healing, and I had nowhere else to turn.

Finally, I gave up. I went to the Lord, who seemed so far removed from me, and relinquished everything to Him. I told

Him, "If I am always going to be this way, then I am Yours. You will have to show me how to serve You. I have all these limitations, but I am still Yours." That day He responded clearly in my spirit: "Good! Now I am going to heal *all* of you, the whole woman." From that point on, it was just Jesus and me.

Psalm 107:20 (NASB) says, "He sent His word and healed them, and delivered them from their destructions." A wise friend of mine suggested that I make a tape for myself, including all the scriptures and lessons I could think of that dealt with my situation. I did, and as I walked daily, listening to the tape, lines of hymns and portions of Scripture came to my mind. My own words spoke truth to me.

The piano I had ignored once again became a blessing to me. I *wanted* to play. God was speaking to me! I knew it. I knew I would be completely healed, so I discontinued all my medications. I never needed them again.

During this time I asked Jim, who had been with me every step of the way, to restore an old slipper chest that had belonged to my mother. It was battered and beaten and had been set aside. The bottom was out, and it was unhinged because things that were too heavy had been placed in it. The wood was scratched and dull.

Jim put a new base on it and stripped and sanded the finish, making the rough places smooth. The beauty of the wood gleamed with its new polish. Now I could again place my favorite treasures in it.

In many ways, I am like that slipper chest. I have stored many treasures from my experience in my spirit. Isaiah 26:13–14 is a scripture that was particularly meaningful to me: "O LORD our God, masters besides You have had dominion over us; but by You only we make mention of Your name. They are dead, they will not live; they are deceased, they will not rise. Therefore You have punished and destroyed them, and made all their memory to perish" (NKJV). And 2 Corinthians 4:7 says, "But we have this treasure in earthen vessels, that the excellence of the power may be of God and not of us" (NKJV).

I could not heal myself. I could only speak God's truth to my body, soul, and spirit. It was the power of God that restored me. It was His power that gave me my life back so I could live to write a new story.

Elizabeth's Legacy

If the measure of finishing well extends to the legacy we imprint on the lives of others, there is perhaps no greater example than Elizabeth. We met her husband, Zechariah, earlier when the angel Gabriel visited him in the temple. The last words we read about Zechariah were "he went home" (Luke 1:23). I can only imagine the scene when he walked through the door. He left able to speak and returned mute. His encounter with the angel had to have shown on his face. He and Elizabeth knew God was going to do something extraordinary, but how and how soon? They had no idea what God was going to do, and neither do we. That is the wonder of living in the new stories God is writing! Watch how God uses these two people, who were technically "too old" to achieve what He had in mind for them: "Later, Zechariah's wife, Elizabeth, became pregnant and did not go out of her house for five months. Elizabeth said, 'Look what the Lord has done for me! My people were ashamed of me, but now the Lord has taken away that shame'" (vv. 24–25).

Elizabeth knew her new story had come straight from the Lord. She and Zechariah were both physically way too old to bear a child, but if it was what the Lord wanted, she knew it would happen. But wait! Zechariah and Elizabeth were not the only ones in their story to receive news they did not expect.

> During Elizabeth's sixth month of pregnancy, God sent the angel Gabriel to Nazareth, a town in Galilee, to a virgin. She was engaged to marry a man named Joseph from the family of David. Her name was Mary. The angel came to her and said, "Greetings! The Lord has blessed you and is with you."
>
> But Mary was very startled by what the angel said and wondered what this greeting might mean. (vv. 26–29)

The angel told Mary not to be afraid. Then he revealed to her that she would become pregnant, and her child would be none other than the Son of God. The Son of God! Can you even imagine how that news must have slapped her in the face? *She* was going to be the mother of the Son of God! Shocked. Overwhelmed. Terrified. Thrilled. Then logically skeptical:

> Mary said to the angel, "How will this happen since I am a virgin?"
>
> The angel said to Mary, "The Holy Spirit will come upon you, and the power of the Most High will cover you. For this reason the baby will be holy and will be called the Son of God. Now Elizabeth, your relative, is also pregnant with a son though she is very old. Everyone thought she could not have

a baby, but she has been pregnant for six months. God can do anything!"

Mary said, "I am the servant of the Lord. Let this happen to me as you say!" Then the angel went away. (vv. 34–38)

Don't you know it was a comfort for Mary to have Elizabeth to turn to for advice? Not only was Elizabeth her relative, but she was also in the same situation as Mary. Although Elizabeth was very old and Mary was very young, they both had become servants in the hands of God to accomplish a task that only He could do. Their situations were wonderful and terrifying at the same time.

When we are living in the middle of a story we may not have planned, isn't it a sweet comfort to find another woman who has gone through or is going through the same thing? We do not live in a vacuum. Although Elizabeth and Mary were in totally unique situations, they had a common place to share their wonder and awe. The first thing Mary did when she heard the news about her pregnancy was to go to Elizabeth.

Mary got up and went quickly to a town in the hills of Judea. She came to Zechariah's house and greeted Elizabeth. When Elizabeth heard Mary's greeting, the unborn baby inside her jumped, and Elizabeth was filled with the Holy Spirit. She cried out in a loud voice, "God has blessed you more than any other woman, and he has blessed the baby to which you will give birth. Why has this good thing happened to me, that the mother of my Lord comes to me? When I heard your voice, the baby inside me jumped with joy. You are blessed because you believed that what the Lord said to you would really happen."

Then Mary said,
"My soul praises the Lord;
my heart rejoices in God my Savior,
because he has shown his concern for his humble
　　servant girl.
From now on, all people will say that I am blessed,
because the Powerful One has done great things for me.
His name is holy." (vv. 39–49)

Can you imagine the scene when these two women met? Oh, to have been in the corner when Mary walked into Zechariah's house, and Elizabeth shouted with joy! (Remember, dear Zechariah could not speak. All he could do was watch and stare in awe at what God was doing.) And did you notice the contrast between Zechariah and Mary? Zechariah doubted God, and he became speechless for nine months. Mary believed God, and she made one of the most beautiful praise speeches in all of Scripture.

The Bible continues Elizabeth's story by saying, "Mary stayed with Elizabeth for about three months and then returned home" (v. 56). It would seem very likely that, considering the times mentioned in Luke, Elizabeth gave birth to John very shortly after Mary went back to Nazareth. Take in this scene and relish what happens.

When it was time for Elizabeth to give birth, she had a boy. Her neighbors and relatives heard how good the Lord was to her, and they rejoiced with her.

When the baby was eight days old, they came to circumcise him. They wanted to name him Zechariah because this was his father's name, but his mother said, "No! He will be named John."

The people said to Elizabeth, "But no one in your family has this name." Then they made signs to his father to find out what he would like to name him. (vv. 57–62)

I always enjoy the picture of what was going on at John's birth. The people were very *into* this birth. They reminded his mother that there was no one named John in her family, as if she did not know it. "Then they made signs to his father" (v. 62). Made signs? Zechariah was not deaf; he was just mute. Oh, the reality of the Scriptures—always so much human interest.

"Zechariah asked for a writing tablet and wrote, 'His name is John,' and everyone was surprised" (v. 63). But why? Elizabeth had already told them his name was to be John. And now notice what happened when Zechariah confirmed God's command:

Immediately Zechariah could talk again, and he began praising God. All their neighbors became alarmed, and in all the mountains of Judea people continued talking about all these things. The people who heard about them wondered, saying, "What will this child be?" because the Lord was with him. (vv. 64–66)

That was a good question. What *would* that child be? Little did they know how strange he would seem to them when he grew up. If they wondered about him when he was born, wait until you see their reaction to him as a young man wearing peculiar clothes and eating weird food (Matt. 3:4).

> *Then Zechariah, John's father, was filled with the Holy*
>   *Spirit and prophesied:*
> *"Let us praise the Lord, the God of Israel,*
>   *because he has come to help his people and has given*
>   *them freedom.*
> *He has given us a powerful Savior*
>   *from the family of God's servant David." (vv. 67–69)*

Zechariah gave a beautiful prophecy to his fellow Israelites who had gathered for the circumcision of his son. Then he spoke a prophecy over John:

> *"Now you, child, will be called a prophet of the Most High God.*
>   *You will go before the Lord to prepare his way."*

> And so the child grew up and became strong in spirit. John lived in the desert until the time when he came out to preach to Israel. (vv. 76, 80)

Then John appeared on the scene as the forerunner of his cousin, Jesus, the Christ. He did not have an easy role, but when asked about the One who was coming behind him and gaining attention and popularity, John said, "I am really happy. He must become greater, and I must become less important" (John 3:29–30).

Go and Tell John

Rather than trying to take the glory for himself, John remained in his own godly role—the one to prepare the way for Jesus—and that

role carried with it serious consequences. The religious leaders—
the ones he called snakes—had thrown him in prison. So John sent
his followers to ask Jesus, "Are you the One who is to come?"

> Jesus answered them, "Go tell John what you hear and see:
> The blind can see, the crippled can walk, and people with skin
> diseases are healed. The deaf can hear, the dead are raised to
> life, and the Good News is preached to the poor. Those who
> do not stumble in their faith because of me are blessed . . . I
> tell you the truth, John the Baptist is greater than any other
> person ever born, but even the least important person in the
> kingdom of heaven is greater than John." (Matt. 11:4–6, 11)

Elizabeth's Significant Legacy

In a situation where many women might have turned to anger
or bitterness, Elizabeth lived above her circumstances to the end
and, by doing so, passed on a legacy of hope that has extended
into the lives of people down through the ages. Imagine, as a
mother, having the Lord and Savior of the world say that *your
son* is "greater than any other person ever born"! It just doesn't get
any better than that.

Elizabeth thought she was living the final chapters of her old
story when Gabriel came to announce that she would have a son.
That same day her *new* story began, and she took it up with joy
and anticipation. Was she old? Yes. But was there more story to
write? Oh, yes! So *much* more! And Elizabeth continued to write
her new story for as long as she lived—a story that lives on today
as one of the most important stories in all of history.

Personal Reflection

1. What do you personally admire most about Elizabeth? Why?
2. How do you think Elizabeth felt, at her advanced age, when she found out she was pregnant? Describe.
3. If Gabriel came to you with similar news, do you think you would react with Zechariah's doubt or Mary's faith? Why?
4. What do you think it will take for you to finish well? Explain.
5. What kind of legacy do you see yourself passing on?
6. Is it the legacy you would *choose*, or do you need to make some adjustments in how you are living today so your life will be a better influence on others' tomorrows?
7. What is the most important lesson you have learned for your life from Elizabeth's legacy?

Journal Entry

To continue your new story; complete the following starter sentence in your personal journal. Then continue writing thoughts and feelings from your heart as long as you need to.

I really want to leave a significant legacy behind someday, and I can begin that new story by . . .

Group Discussion Questions

1. Both John and Jesus came from the tribe of Judah. What family values must that tribe have instilled in their young women to have them chosen by God for such important roles?

2. Why did Mary travel to see Elizabeth after she found out they were both pregnant? And why did she stay so long?

3. We often criticize Zechariah for doubting God, but what are some reasons Zechariah probably questioned what Gabriel told him?

4. How did John view himself in relationship to Jesus?

5. How did John's view mirror Elizabeth's view in Luke 1?

6. How did Jesus describe John the Baptist?

7. Why did Jesus say John was the *greatest* man ever born, but he was not as important as the *least* person in the kingdom of God? Are these statements contradictory?

8. What is the legacy that Elizabeth left by leaving her old story behind and writing a new story?

Conclusion

SAME LIFE, NEW STORY

You cannot not tell your story!

—original author unknown

Naomi, Leah, Rahab, Deborah, Hannah, Anna, Jehosheba, Abigail, Naaman's servant girl, and Elizabeth. All of these remarkable women were living old stories when we met them. And each of them, in her own way and for her own reasons, could have easily just decided to stay right where she was. Don't take risks. Don't make waves. Don't give up what is comfortable. And yet not one of them did that, and the life-altering results, the influence on generations to come, have been powerful.

Is it always easy to leave your old story behind and begin writing a new one? By *no* means. But is it worth it? By *all* means! A new story often gives you a new lease on life. It adds excitement, a new view of the future, hope, and anticipation. It gives you a new reason to live beyond your old story—to reach forward in your life rather than constantly looking backward. God does not mean for us to live life looking in the rearview mirror. The result is always disastrous. Looking forward gives you the greater chance of heading in the right direction.

If you're tired of doing life the same old way, or if what you are doing just isn't working anymore, you *can* change . . . starting today! It's a choice you get to make. Today, begin creating the legacy you really want to leave behind for generations to read and remember about you. "You cannot *not* tell your story," and you have the great privilege of deciding the story you want to tell.

The way to begin is to recognize it is time. It's not too early or too late. Today is the day. Then turn to God to help you. Just tell Him you are ready to move on even if you do not know how or what to do about it. He will give you the plan, although it will often be in small steps. Remember to keep your eyes on the bigger story—God's plan for you—and do not get bogged down in the smaller dramas that keep you distracted. They are part of your story, but not the most important part. If you look in the rearview mirror, you will see them, but they are behind you. Why not leave them there and move on to something bigger and better? You will be leaving a legacy of joy and hope.

God is waiting for you to join Him in His story. As you catch a glimpse of what He has planned for you, I believe you will willingly pick up your pen and begin to write. You will live the same life, but you will write a new story!

> "I know what I am planning for you . . . I have *good* plans for you, not plans to hurt you. I will give you hope and a *good future*. When you search for me with all your heart, you will find me! I will *let* you find me," says the LORD. (Jer. 29:11, 13–14, italics mine)

Notes

Introduction: If You Change Your Story, You Can Change Your Life

1. Louisa Fletcher, *The Land of Beginning Again* (Boston, MA: Small, Maynard and Company, 1921).

Chapter 1: Realize It's Time to Get a Life and Tell a New Story

1. Listening to the teaching of Kay Arthur for fourteen years, I have heard her make this statement in repeated messages.

Chapter 2: Don't Be Held Hostage by the Past

1. Dan Baker and Cameron Stauth, *What Happy People Know* (New York: St. Martin's Press, 2003), 148.

Chapter 4: Change Your "I Can't" to "I Can"

1. Martin Seligman, *Learned Helplessness: A Theory for the Age of Personal Control* (New York: Oxford University Press, 1995).

2. Ibid., 121.

3. Ibid.

4. Dan Baker and Cameron Stauth, *What Happy People Know* (New York: St. Martin's Press, 2003), 122–123.

5. Spiros Zodhiates, ThD, *Hebrew-Greek Key Word Study Bible* (Chattanooga, TN: AMG International, 2008), 327.

6. David Ray Smith, *The Tennessee Encyclopedia of History and Culture* (Nashville: The Tennessee Historical Society, 1998).

7. Ibid.

8. Rowena McClinton, ed. and translator, *The Moravian Springplace Mission to the Cherokees*, vol. 1, 1805–1813 (Lincoln, NE: University of Nebraska Press, 2007).

9. D. I. Bock, *The New American Commentary, Judges, Ruth*, vol. 6 (electronic ed.), Logos Library System (Nashville: Broadman & Holman Publishers, 2001).

Chapter 5: Delete the Drama of the Day

1. Macrina Wiederkehr, *Behold Your Life: A Pilgrimage Thru Your Memories* (Notre Dame, IN: Ave Maria Press, 2000), 119.

Chapter 7: Discover the Power of Wisdom and Courage Combined

1. Irene Opdyke, *Into My Hands: Memories of a Holocaust Rescuer* (Harpswell, ME: Anchor, 1999, 2001).

Chapter 8: Get Past the Resistance of Fear

1. An ancient adage. First recorded by Dutch scholar Desiderius Erasmus (1466–1536) in *Adagia*.

2. For more information about dealing with fools, see the author's *Fool-proofing Your Life: How to Deal Effectively with the Impossible People in Your Life* (Colorado Springs, CO: Waterbrook, 2009).

3. Edna St. Vincent Millay (1892–1950), "Ashes of Life," *Renascence and Other Poems* (Ithaca, NY: Cornell University Library, 2010).

Chapter 9: Choose to Bounce Back

1. Amy Carmichael, *Candles in the Dark* (Fort Washington, PA: Christian Literature Crusade, 1981), 90. Used by permission.

2. June Scobee Rodgers, *Silver Linings: Triumph of Challenger 7* (Peake Road Publications, 1996). Used by permission.

3. Ibid., 87.

4. Ibid., 112.

5. Anna Quindlen, *A Short Guide to a Happy Life* (New York: Random House, 2000), 45. Used by permission.

6. Dan Baker and Cameron Stauth, *What Happy People Know* (New York: St. Martin's Press, 2003), 148.

Chapter 10: The Last Chapter Has Not Been Written Yet!

1. Walter Bortz, as quoted by Dan Baker, *What Happy People Know* (New York: St. Martin's Press, 2003).

LEAVE LITTLE-GIRL WAYS BEHIND AND BECOME THE STRONG, MATURE, CONFIDENT WOMAN GOD INTENDS YOU TO BE!

No one wants to be labeled a whiner, but many of us go through life with a poor-me victim mentality that sounds a whole lot like whining. God never intended for us to act like "little girls," says Jan Silvious. His goal is for each of us to live as "big girls"—mature Christian women—who are capable of enjoying the richness of life He has planned. In *Big Girls Don't Whine* . . .

ISBN 13: 978-0-8499-4441-3

• Choose to be proactive
• Move beyond the past and on to healthy relationships
• Discover your full potential

ISBN 13: 978-0-7852-2815-8

Jan gives savvy advice to help you deal with the important choices you face every day, realizing the value of the second look, the second perspective, and the second consideration as well as the significance of acknowledging red flags.

Smart Girls Think Twice is biblically sound, psychologically positive wisdom for smart choices in eight critical areas, including Words, Men, Giving, and Rest.

Wherever books are sold or at *ThomasNelson.com*

THOMAS NELSON
Since 1798